HOW TO WIN OVER

Worry

A practical formula for successful living

JOHN HAGGAI

HARVEST HOUSE PUBLISHERS
Eugene, Oregon 97402

Scripture quotations in this book are taken from the King James Version of the Bible.

HOW TO WIN OVER WORRY

Copyright © 1987 by Harvest House Publishers
Eugene, Oregon 97402

Library of Congress Catalog Card Number 87-081667
ISBN 0-89081-574-7 (Trade Edition)
ISBN 0-89081-643-3 (Cloth Edition)

Printed in the United States of America.

Contents

Part 4 — PRAYER

Part 5 — PEACE

Preface

Every time I write an article for a magazine or a manuscript for a book, I grapple with the problem of worry—the divided mind. Will some of the statements come back to haunt me 20 years from now? Will the views expressed subject me to the ridicule of my peers? Will statements made be misunderstood by sincere people with the result that they will suffer hurt, though my aim was to help? Will some of the readers conclude the material was superficial and frivolous? Will I, after the publication of the book, conclude that the hours and energy and, yes, emotional pain, invested in producing the manuscript didn't pay off; rather that it turned out to be a travesty of productive enterprise? Will the publisher give the book fair exposure?

The initial edition of *How to Win Over Worry* (1959) got very little attention from the publisher. In less than two years, the publisher's sales representative announced to bookstore owner Bob Hawkins the publisher's intention not to reprint the book after the present edition was exhausted. Bob Hawkins owned two bookstores in Oregon at the time. He said, "That book cannot go out of print." In vigorous terms he gave reasons why it must be reprinted. To prove his point of the book's importance, he ordered 500 hardback copies. Some people would think that an order of 500 hardback copies for two modest-sized bookstores in a modest-sized city would be foolhardy. Bob sold them all within two months.

What Bob Hawkins did for that book got it off the ground. Had I known of the publisher's plan at the time to not reprint my book, I'm sure I never would have written another book. Since Bob's purchase of those 500 copies of the book, it has now been translated into 18 languages and gone through more than 50 printings. I am pleased that this man and his family own the company, Harvest House, that is publishing this new and expanded version of *How to Win Over Worry*.

Just last night my brother Tom called to tell me that a lady under psychiatric care had been given a copy of this book. When she went to the psychiatrist he told her she was doing much better and asked how she accounted for it. She told him she didn't know. He then asked if she had done anything differently. She simply mentioned that she had read the book *How to Win Over Worry*. He asked to see it. He has now ordered a supply because he wants to give the book to some of his patients.

One of the South's prominent business tycoons saw me at the airport in San Antonio, Texas, early one morning. He asked if I was John Haggai. I said yes. He then told me how God had used that book to avert his suicide at the very moment he had the .38 revolver to his temple ready to blow out his brains. His daughter had picked up a copy of the book in London. It helped her so much she wanted her father to read it too, so she left it on his bedside table.

God used the book to avert the planned suicide of one of London's highy publicized and world-famous impresarios. A friend of his asked me to autograph a copy for this impresario. On the day when he was ready to pull the trigger of the suicide gun, he heard a thud. He went to the upstairs railing across from his bedroom to see what caused the noise. He looked down to see the postman had pushed a parcel through the slot. He opened the package, saw my book, read it, found meaning for his life, then placed a transatlantic phone call to thank me.

The internationally renowned Dr. Paul Yonggi Cho, founder and pastor of the world's largest church (membership over 600,000), came to my hotel in 1970 and told me that ten years earlier God had used the book *How to Win Over Worry* to meet his deep needs during the time of sickness and depression. When I saw him ten years later, he told me he had preached from the book on several occasions.

The late Mr. Stanley Kresge told me that he and his wife had read one chapter of *How to Win Over Worry* each morning, along with their other devotional materials, during their quiet time until they finished the 25 chapters of the book.

I read it periodically myself, since I need it. I did not create the ideas. I simply put down the truths that I found.

It encourages me greatly to know that this volume has sold over half a million copies in the United States and, in abridged form, three times that number overseas. The writings have crossed the threshold of hundreds of thousands of homes I shall never visit, and the influence of this book will touch the lives of millions of people I'll never meet. Despite all that encouragement, I still must keep my guard up against the monster of worry.

Reading this book through once and agreeing with its principles will not eliminate worry. I suggest that you read it and reread it. Make notes in the margins or inside the back cover of passages that have special relevance to your need. Write out specific goals with time targets to cope with your problems relating to worry. Devote the first moments of every day to reading the Bible. This is more important to your mastery of worry than reading any other book.

The formula for winning over worry is **Praise** plus **Poise** plus **Prayer** equals **Perfect Peace**. You must win over worry before you can master any worthwhile undertaking in life.

I pray this book will encourage you to work toward the mastery of worry and thus to move toward your potential.

Should you have questions about anything I've written, please write me at Box 13, Atlanta, Georgia 30370. I will answer your query. God bless you.

Part 1

SURVEYING THE PROBLEM

1

Meet Public Enemy Number One

You can die of worry.

It's not a cancer. It's not caused by a virus. If you're afflicted by it no doctor in his right mind would say you are physically ill. Nonetheless worry is a potentially fatal condition.

And it's spreading. Let me introduce you to an astounding and terrifying fact: According to Mike Gorman, the Executive Director of the National Mental Health Committee, half of all hospital beds in the United States are occupied by people suffering mental disturbance. Half! And in his book *Every Other Bed* he predicts that in the near future the proportion will rise to two thirds. That means two out of every three hospital places are taken up by the victims of mental illness, at a cost of billions of dollars a year.

Listen to the *Supplement to the American Journal of Psychiatry,* July 1985, in a report titled "Research on Mental Illness and Addictive Disorders: Progress and Prospects":

> In the United States, 15 percent to 22.5 percent of the population has some form of mental illness . . .
>
> One percent of the population will develop Schizophrenia. Over 9 million currently have affective disorders. Five percent of the population suffers from generalized anxiety. Ten million adults and three million children abuse alcohol, and millions of individuals abuse drugs.
>
> Major mental disorders, alcoholism and drug addiction disrupt the lives of 32 to 45 million people in the United States each year.

Take the lowest estimate in that report—15 percent suffering some form of mental illness. Reckoning on the basis of the

1980 census figure of 226,545,805, that means 33,981,870 people. In other words the number of mentally disturbed in America today exceeds the entire population of Canada. The root cause? Worry!

Look at the statistics on suicide in the United States. In 1972 24,280 people committed suicide. By 1982 the figure had risen to 28,200. Now the 1987 *Information Please Almanac* states that "suicide claims the lives of at least thirty thousand Americans annually." At a conservative estimate that's over 6,000 more suicides per year today than 15 years ago. Statistically speaking you're more likely to kill yourself than you are to be killed by someone else.

And of course killing yourself doesn't just mean jumping off a bridge. The evidence has piled up over recent years that worry causes death through a wide range of physical disorders. In 1982 6,700 people died as a result of ulcers in the stomach and duodenum. And that's just ulcers. We were shocked in World War II to hear that a third of a million of America's finest young people had been killed in combat. But did you know that, over exactly the same period, one million—three times as many people—died of heart disease right where they were in the USA?

Read the excellent book by Dr. Edward Podolsky, *Stop Worrying and Get Well*. It deals with the correlation between worry and heart trouble, worry and blood pressure, worry and rheumatism, ulcers, colds, thyroid malfunction, arthritis, migraine headaches, blindness, and a host of stomach disorders. The fact is that worry causes any number of physical malfunctions, and those malfunctions can kill. Dr. Alexis Carroll spelled it out to one group of worriers: "Businessmen who don't know how to fight worry die young," he said.

Is worry a problem that only afflicts top-level executives? Not on your life! People from every echelon of society worry. A leading physician has stated that 70 percent of all medical patients could cure themselves if only they got rid of their fears and worries—he knew, because he'd suffered a stomach ulcer for exactly that reason. Or take the testimony of two outstanding doctors who set up the Medical Arts Clinic in Corsicana, Texas. They told me that the first complaint of more than 70 percent of their patients is: "Doctor, I can't sleep." Why? Worry!

Let me give you an example of the effect of worry.

Several years ago a pastor friend of mine, Eddie Lieberman, was asked to try and help a young lady apparently suffering severe depression. He went to see her. She told him she was sick, that she didn't love her husband anymore (he was overseas in the Armed Forces at the time), and that she wanted a divorce. Her physical state was deteriorating badly, and in fact she soon became a total paralytic.

Besides being a pastor, Eddie Lieberman is trained as a psychologist. He declined an invitation to become the first case psychologist in one of our leading Baptist hospitals only because he wanted to pursue his first calling—to the gospel ministry. And his instincts as a psychologist told him something was drastically wrong with this girl, so he requested permission to admit her to Duke University Hospital.

There she confessed to her psychiatrist that she'd received a letter from her husband telling her he'd fallen in love with another girl. It was he, not she, who wanted to initiate divorce proceedings. She had never told anyone about this, but bottling it up had caused severe anxiety, and anxiety had led to paralysis. Eddie Lieberman tried to help her, but it is almost impossible to help someone who fundamentally has no desire to be helped. She refused to face the facts. Today, when she should be a lively, vivacious woman in her mid-thirties, she is a morose paralytic bound for a premature grave. The culprit: Worry.

Worry is not a disease. But it causes disease. And like a disease, it is contagious—in fact several outstanding psychiatrists believe it is more contagious than scarlet fever or diptheria. So much so that in the West today, and particularly in the United States, people worry about worry. Pick up a popular magazine and you are likely to find an article about stress or anxiety. "How to Face Your Fears, Tensions and

Worries" was a headline I read in the *Pageant* not so long ago. *Reader's Digest* for the same week devoted eight and a half pages to the subject of "The Inner Secret of Health." It seems we have an almost obsessive desire to get rid of our worry. Worry is public enemy number one.

How does worry work?

The New Testament word for worry is translated "take thought" and "be careful". J. B. Phillips correctly translates it "worry."

The word "worry" comes from the Greek word *merimnao* which is a combination of two words: *merizo* meaning "to divide" and *nous* meaning "mind" (including the faculties of perceiving, understanding, feeling, judging, and determining).

Worry, then, means "to divide the mind." Worry divides the mind between worthwhile interests and damaging thoughts.

The apostle James states the unhappy condition of the person with the divided mind:

> A double minded man is unstable in all his ways (James 1:8).

You will notice that James says that the man with the divided mind is unstable in *all his ways*. He is unstable in his emotions. He is unstable in his thought processes. He is unstable in his decisions. He is unstable in his judgments.

Peace of mind requires singleness of mind. The worrier robs himself of peace of mind by dividing his mind.

Worry divides the feelings, therefore the emotions lack stability.

Worry divides the understanding, therefore convictions are shallow and changeable.

Worry divides the faculty of perception, therefore observations are faulty and even false.

Worry divides the faculty of judging, therefore attitudes and decisions are often unjust. These decisions lead to damage and grief.

Worry divides the determinative faculty, therefore plans and purposes, if not "scrapped" altogether, are not fulfilled with persistence.

Worry in the extreme leads to *abulia*—loss of the power to will. Why? The mind is so divided it cannot act in one channel. It is like the mule who stood between two haystacks and starved to death trying to decide from which stack to eat.

Abulia is often termed a "nervous breakdown." In such a breakdown, pressures have so built up as a result of divided-mindedness that the victim ceases struggling with his problems and responds in a depressed and passive manner.

Worry is the cause of heartbreak, failure, misunderstanding, suspicion, and most unhappiness.

Is there any home which has gone "on the rocks" that cannot point to "the divided mind" as the cause? It may be that the husband's mind was divided between the wife and another woman. It may be that the wife divided her mind between the husband and "Mama." Her mind may have been divided between an inexcusably possessive preoccupation with her children and her God-ordained responsibilities to her husband. It may be that the mind was divided between home responsibilities and selfish, personal desires. It may be that the husband divided his mind between an inordinate ambition to succeed and his responsibilities as husband and father. With just a little thought you can come readily to many other possibilities or certainties which have divided the mind and wrecked the home.

Who can determine the percentage of school failures effectuated by "the divided mind"? Preachers' sons, believe it or not, confront difficulties in their youth. That goes for preachers' daughters as well. If they are "model children," the parents of other children hold them up as a pattern of behavior with the result that their friends detest them. If, on the other hand, they are normally mischievous, the other children appreciate them and their parents detest them. I have a brother who was so sensitive to the fact that he was a preacher's son that he deliberately made poor grades so the kids wouldn't think of him as a "goody-goody." Worry ruined his grades. He has an excellent mind. This fact has since been proven by his collegiate scholastic records. He graduated with honors in a difficult field from one of the nation's leading universities.

Do not some children fail in school because of discord in the home—discord that divides their minds between their scholastic responsibilities and the possible outcome of the domestic "cold war"? Do not some children bungle their school opportunities simply because they are neglected at home? They feel unwanted and therefore they create havoc at school in order to get the attention that they do not get at home.

Only the Lord knows how many businesses have been torpedoed by worry—the divided mind. There was a man who opened a hot-dog stand. His business grew. He expanded. Soon he had a chain of stands. He was making fabulous money. He sent his son to college. The son graduated with a major in Business Administration. This was in 1933. The father took him into the business. The son said, "You know, Dad, there's a depression on. Business is bad everywhere. Many businesses have gone into bankruptcy. We must be careful. Let's cut down our inventory, reduce our advertising budget, lay off some of the help, and tighten our belts." The father listened to his "learned" son and followed the advice reluctantly. Yes, you've guessed it. The son succeeded in dividing his father's mind between the principles of success and the potential threats of the depression. Soon their business folded. Worse yet, depressed by the financial reverses, the father lost his sparkle, his "drive," his optimistic outlook and began to deteriorate physically.

One of the best-known tycoons of our nation during this century made and then lost three huge fortunes. Why? Because he over and over again divided his mind between his business interests and "gold-digging" paramours.

One of the most bitter and cynical men I have ever known was a man loaded with talent. He had more ability than six typical men. He could have been a leading cartoonist, or a top-notch photographer, or a highly paid after-dinner speaker, or a humorist, or a prosperous realtor, or a topflight hotel executive, or a celebrated writer. He never amounted to anything. He saw men who obviously did not possess one fraction of his ability soar to the heights of success while he groveled in the mud. Those who knew him well knew the reason. It was a divided mind. He never came to the point at which he determined what he was going to do. He could not say with Paul the apostle, "This one thing I do." He would never throw all of his energies in a single project. He aimed at nothing, hit a bull's-eye, and then brooded over the result. He became critical of others who did achieve. With unparalleled cynicism he would rationalize his failure and deal out misery to all of his associates. His health broke completely. A distraught mind inevitably leads to a deteriorated body.

Worry is ravaging societies worldwide. It is slaying tens of thousands of people. It is infiltrating businesses and bringing them crashing down. It's passing through homes like a tornado, leaving in its wake bitter and frustrated parents, and insecure, terrified children. It is driving some to spend fortunes on psychotherapy, and heading others into psychiatric care. In America at least, it has virtually become part of the national culture. You could write on countless American gravestones the epitaph: *Hurried, Worried, Buried.*

So you're worried. It's your problem too. Worry is your personal enemy as well as a public enemy. But what are you going to do about it?

Well, there are many solutions to worry. Of those solutions, I assure you confidently, there is *only one that works*—the one presented by God in the Bible. I will be giving the formula for that solution in chapter 3. But in case you don't believe me when I say it's the only effective solution, take a look first of all at the other ways worriers try to cope with their problem.

2

Throw Away Your Popgun

A popgun is a fine toy for children. It gives them action and noise. It arrests their attention—for a time, at least. When a boy arrives at the age of adolescence, he no longer finds much interest in a popgun. And could there be anything more ludicrous and incongruous than a full-grown man whiling away his time shooting a little dime store popgun?

You cannot kill a bear or a lion or any vicious enemy of human life with a popgun. Men do not go hunting with popguns. Nor are soldiers equipped with popguns when called upon to fight an enemy.

Shooting a popgun probably takes as much effort as shooting a .22-caliber rifle or many other types of guns. Some popguns make as much noise as real guns. Apart from occupying the attention for a little while, making some noise, and requiring the exertion of some effort, popguns accomplish nothing.

The majority of worriers try to kill this vicious enemy, worry, with popguns. Figuratively speaking, that is. Let us mention a few of the more prominent popguns that are used.

There is the popgun of *flattery*. Flattery is a device used by many seeking to compensate for worry. By flattery the worrier endeavors to secure loyal friends in large numbers. He thereby seeks to immunize himself from danger by building around himself this wall of friends. It is his thought that there is safety in numbers. He reasons that if the dreadful probabilities he fears become calamitous certainties, he will be shielded by this wall of friends.

Obviously flattery accomplishes nothing except to give a temporary and a false security to the flatterer. The very dishonesty of this attempt ultimately adds to the worries of the worrier.

21

Flattery is mentioned and denounced over 30 times in the Word of God. Job says:

> He that speaketh flattery to his friends, even the eyes of his children shall fail (Job 17:5).

Again in Job:

> Let me not, I pray you, accept any man's person, neither let me give flattering titles unto man.
> For I know not to give flattering titles; in so doing my maker would soon take me away (Job 32:21,22).

The psalmist records the sinfulness and foolishness of flattery in Psalm 5:9:

> For there is no faithfulness in their mouth . . .
> they flatter with their tongue.

You remember the statement made in the previous chapter that worry is essentially divided-mindedness. Notice now how that fits in with the following words of the psalmist:

> They speak vanity every one with his neighbor; with flattering lips and with a *double heart* do they speak (Psalm 12:2).

The wisest man of history, Solomon, admonishes us:

> He that goeth about as a talebearer revealeth secrets: therefore meddle not with him that flattereth with his lips (Proverbs 20:19).

> A lying tongue hateth those that are afflicted by it; and a flattering mouth worketh ruin (Proverbs 26:28).

Another popgun utilized by many worriers is that of *criticism*. Psychologists tell us there are three reasons for this.

First, we criticize to elevate ourselves. Second, we criticize to project our miserableness. Third, we criticize the very thing of which we are guilty, or the thing which tempts us and troubles us the most.

No matter what may be your motive for criticism, the old saying is true, "It doesn't take much size to criticize."

Remember that popguns are used only by children and the popgun of criticism, like the other figurative popguns mentioned in this chapter, is used by the most immature personalities.

Worriers often resort to criticism to project their own miserableness. They are miserable and they want everyone else to be miserable. This obviously is not the answer to worry. In thus projecting their own misery, people succeed temporarily in getting their minds off their own problems. The tragic result, however, is that the relief is only temporary. In criticizing they are focusing their minds upon negative thoughts, and the mischief that inevitably follows negative thinking but adds to their worries. Consequently the depression becomes more intense.

It is true that "what Peter says about Paul tells more about Peter than it does about Paul." Or, in the words of the little couplet:

Things that thou dost in others see, are the most prevalent in thee.

The Bible tells us that to the impure, all things are impure (Titus 1:15). To the dishonest, all are dishonest. To the untrue, all are untrue. When the worrier criticizes others, he certainly solves none of his own worries. He focuses his attention upon the miserable traits he sees in others which mirror his own condition. His mind is riveted to this destructively negative thinking in such a way that more fear-producing thoughts are bred to add to his already overstocked supply of fears.

Paul the apostle denounces the sin of criticism when in Romans 2:1 he says:

> Therefore thou art inexcusable, O man, whatso-
> ever thou art that judgest: for wherein thou judgest
> another, thou condemnest thyself; for thou that
> judgest doest the same things.

What the worrier fails to realize is that in criticizing others he is revealing to the world what he himself is.

Another popgun that many worriers use in their endeavor to kill this vicious enemy of worry is that of *excessive activity*. This is only a temporary escape. Through this means they try in vain to conquer their worries, but they only postpone their misery with a temporary emotional intoxication. They think they are busy when they are only "nervous." (Later on you will understand why I put the word "nervous" in quotes.) They are like a worm on a hot rock. As one TV personality said, "They are as nervous as a long-tailed cat in a room full of rocking chairs." Spinning their wheels, they are going nowhere. They seem to have become infatuated with the twentieth-century beatitude, "Blessed are they that go around in circles, for they shall be called big wheels."

This feverish activity, motivated by the desire to escape rather than the urge to produce, solves no problems. It simply takes the mind for a brief spell off the fear-producing thoughts that cause the anxiety. This type of activity, instead of solving problems, actually produces more problems and thereby intensifies the problem over which victory is sought.

It is amazing how few people can stand their own company for 30 minutes without any action or device such as TV, radio, books, or any other prop. They do not know the meaning of the words of our Lord,

> Come ye yourselves apart into a desert place, and
> rest a while (Mark 6:31).

They take phenobarbital to go to sleep, Dexedrine to get started in the morning, and they stay tanked up on coffee to make it through the day. That which they call fervor is actually no more than emotional fever.

Another popgun used by many worriers in their vain effort to kill this vicious enemy of worry is the popgun of a *self-righteous resignation*. There is nothing righteous about this kind of resignation. You notice I said it is a self-righteous resignation. They will assert, "My cross is heavy, but I am determined to take it valiantly." This is almost blasphemous. Wherever the biblical injunction "take up thy cross" appears, it is referring to death to sin and death to self. This is the exact antithesis of the attitude just referred to. The Bible never refers to any problem, grief, or dilemma as a cross that some people are called to bear. The man who really bears his cross is the man who knows no worry. He has died to sin and to self. Thus he is invulnerable to destructive fears. He has peace because his mind is ever staid upon Christ and because he trusts in Christ.

Jesus never complained about the weight of His cross. However, He bore a cross. A real cross—a cross for you and for me.

Our Lord's disciples rejoiced that "they were counted worthy to suffer shame for His name" (Acts 5:41).

These people who respond to worry, fear, and anxiety with a self-righteous resignation say one thing, but they live another. They delude no one but themselves. Although they claim to want to bring glory to God, their faces would "draw a wart" on a tombstone. They repeat the sin of Jonah who said in Jonah 4:3:

> Therefore now, O Lord, take, I beseech thee, my
> life from me; for it is better for me to die than to live.

And the sin of Elijah:

> . . . It is enough; now, O Lord, take away my life;
> for I am not better than my fathers (1 Kings 19:4c).

This is not spiritual courage. This is disgusting cowardice. It is the most revolting type of self-pity.

Some worriers resort to the popgun of *alcohol* and/or *narcotics* in a vain effort to kill the vicious enemy of worry.

This gives them temporary exhilaration during which their minds may not be focused upon the fear-producing thoughts that cause them so much grief. However, this type of behavior only postpones the problem. It ultimately increases the agony.

Perspective is distorted under the influence of stimulants. This often leads to regrettable circumstances which result in an increase of the problems of the worrier. Who can calculate the damage done by the many plays (whether in book form, staged on Broadway, projected on the television or movie screen) which portray the unrequited lover desperately going down to the corner saloon to drink away his sorrows. The attitude that a drunken spree is the way to escape an agonizing situation produces pernicious results. The Japanese say: "A man takes a drink, then the drink takes a drink, and the next drink takes the man."

Solomon, the sage of the ages, speaks wisely when he says:

> Who hath woe? who hath sorrow? who hath contentions? who hath babbling? who hath wounds without cause? who hath redness of eyes?
> They that tarry long at the wine; they that go to seek mixed wine (Proverbs 23:29,30).

It is still true that:

> Wine is a mocker, strong drink is raging: and whosoever is deceived thereby is not wise (Proverbs 20:1).

Some worriers resort to yet another popgun. They seek to conquer worry by *positive thinking*. Now positive thinking is good. Certainly a person cannot have positive thoughts and fear-producing, worrisome thoughts at the same time. Nevertheless, the worrier needs help from outside—or to be more specific, from above. It is one thing to know what we ought to do. It is another thing to have the ability to do it. The Ten Commandments showed man what he must be and what he must do, but no man—our own Lord, the God-man excepted—has ever kept the Ten Commandments. It is one thing to know what we must be and what we must do, and another to meet the demands.

With all of my heart I believe in the power of positive thinking. Let it be understood, however, that God alone is the source of positive thoughts. Paul says in 2 Timothy 1:7:

> For God hath not given us the spirit of fear; but of power, and of love, and of a sound mind.

Positive thoughts do not constitute a useless "popgun" in this instance. Rather they produce the erroneous concept that man in his own strength can bring about the kind of mental attitude that will banish fear and worry. Man might just as well try to shoot an African lion with a popgun as to conquer his worry with his own self-inspired and self-produced positive attitude.

Later on in the book you will notice that much emphasis is given to positive thinking. Equal emphasis is also made on the basis of human experience and on the basis of God's Word that there is no such thing as peace except to those who have properly related themselves to the Lord Jesus Christ, the Prince of Peace. Apart from divine help, a proper mental attitude—one that gives peace—is totally impossible. A man's belief that he can be the source of a proper mental attitude is a Pollyanna notion that leads ultimately to frustration.

There are many other popguns used to slay the deadly beast, the enemy worry. Those who resort to the use of these various popguns reveal their immaturity and their helplessness. I do not say this disparagingly. God grant that this book will lead them to a proper relationship with God through Christ who is our Peace (cf. Ephesians 2:14). The first requisite for help must be that you *throw away your popgun*.

Thousands of people every year resort to the popgun of *suicide*. It goes without saying this accomplishes nothing. It is like a man cutting off his head to cure the headache.

One of the most heartrending articles I've ever read appeared on the front page of the May 21, 1931 edition of *The New York Times*. This article dealt with the suicide of Ralph Barton. Mr. Barton was an outstanding cartoonist, one of the nation's leading caricaturists. He was highly gifted, a great writer. His life ended tragically by his own hand.

In his suicide note he told about the melancholia he had been suffering. Apparently his fears nearly drove him mad. Read verbatim part of what he said in his suicide note:

> It (melancholia) has prevented my getting anything like the full value out of my talent, and the past three years has made work a torture to do at all. It has made it impossible for me to enjoy the simple pleasures of life.

Now I am taking the liberty of italicizing that part of his note which I want impressed upon you.

> *I have run from wife to wife, from house to house, and from country to country in a ridiculous effort to escape from myself.*In doing so I am very much afraid that I have brought a great deal of unhappiness to those who have loved me . . .
>
> *No one thing is responsible for this and no one person— except myself . . .*
>
> *I did it because I am fed up with inventing devices for getting through the twenty-four hours a day and with bridging over a few months periodically with some beautiful interest. . . .*

Poor fellow. Brilliant of mind! How tragic that a life such as his, filled with great possibilities for blessing his generation in the will of God, had to end in such tragedy!

He tried to kill the stalking lion of worry and melancholia with a series of useless popguns.

Throw away your popgun. This is your first step if you would conquer worry.

3

Worry Is a Sin

Worry is a SIN—a blighting sin that has become the subject matter of nonsensical satire.

Worry cannot be excused as an uncontrollable condition. It's amazing how easy it is to blame our problems on our heredity—our parents, grandparents, and forebears.

I chuckle inside every time somebody says to me, "Worry is not a sin for me; you see, my mother was a worrier and my father was a worrier and, therefore, I am a worrier."

I chuckle because it reminds me of the Vermont Republican zealot:

> A Democrat from the South asked this man living in Republican Vermont, "Why are you a Republican?"
>
> The Vermonter answered, "My father was a Republican, and my grandfather was a Republican, and, therefore, I am a Republican."
>
> The Southerner said, "Suppose your father had been a fool, and your grandfather had been a fool, then what would you be?"
>
> "Oh, in that case, I'd be a Democrat."

You cannot blame your worries on a congenital condition communicated through your blood, a condition inherited from your parents.

Worry is a sin. It is always a sin, and it is a sin for two reasons: Worry is distrust in the truthfulness of God and worry is detrimental to the temple of God.

1. *Worry is distrust in the truthfulness of God.*

When you worry you accuse God of falsehood.

God's Word says, "And we know that all things work together for good to them that love God, to them who are the called according to his purpose" (Romans 8:28). Worry says, "Thou liest, O God!"

God's Word says, "He hath done all things well" (Mark 7:37). Worry says, "Thou liest, O God!"

God's Word says, "I can do all things through Christ which strengtheneth me" (Philippians 4:13). Worry says, "Thou liest, O God!"

God's Word says, "But my God shall supply all your needs according to his riches in glory by Christ Jesus" (Philippians 4:19). Worry says, "Thou liest, O God!"

God's Word says, "I will never leave thee, nor forsake thee" (Hebrews 13:5). Worry says, "Thou liest, O God!"

God's Word says, "He careth for you" (1 Peter 5:7). Worry says, "Thou liest, O God!"

God's Word says, "Take no thought for your life, what ye shall eat, or what ye shall drink; nor yet for your body, what ye shall put on . . . for your heavenly Father knoweth that ye have need of all these things" (Matthew 6:25a, 32b). Worry says, "Thou liest, O God!"

Worry is hypocrisy, for it professes faith in God and at the same time assails the reality of His truthfulness.

If it is highy insulting to call a man a liar (although the fact is that David probably spoke the truth when he said, "All men are liars"), how infinitely more inexcusable it is to accuse the sovereign God of falsehood. He is the God "who cannot lie."

In hope of eternal life, which God, that cannot lie, promised before the world began (Titus 1:2).

He that believeth not God hath made him a liar . . . (1 John 5:10).

2. *Worry is a sin because it is detrimental to the temple of God.*
If a group of vandals should crash into your church some dark night and succeed in shattering the stained-glass windows, ripping up the carpeting, smashing the furniture, wrecking the musical instruments, disfiguring the walls, and ravaging the Sunday school rooms, you would react with

justifiable anger and prosecute them to the full extent of the law. The laws of the land provide stringent penalties for disturbance of public worship and for destruction of church property. You would make the most of these laws, as well you should.

Yet worry is a far more inexcusable and grievous sin than this vandalism of church property. In all probability, these vandals were not professing Christians, while many who worry are. Furthermore, there is no inherent value in a church building. True, it symbolizes worship. It symbolizes the work and the Word of God. However, its only inherent value is symbolic. God does not dwell in the church building as such. He dwells there only as He dwells in the hearts of those who worship there.

God *does* dwell in the heart of every believer.

> Know ye not that ye are the temple of God, and that the Spirit of God dwelleth in you? (1 Corinthians 3:16).

> What? know ye not that your body is the temple of the Holy Ghost which is in you, which ye have of God, and ye are not your own? (1 Corinthians 6:19).

> Ye also, as lively stones, are built up a spiritual house, an holy priesthood, to offer up spiritual sacrifices, acceptable to God by Jesus Christ. (1 Peter 2:5).

> And because ye are sons, God hath sent forth the Spirit of his Son into your hearts . . . (Galatians 4:6).

Worry debilitates and even destroys the temple of God which is *your own body,* Christian! In chapter 1 we mentioned some of the detrimental effects worry has on the body— God's temple. Let's review for a moment. Some of the ailments caused by worry (according to Dr. Edward Podolsky to whom I referred in chapter 1) are heart trouble, high blood pressure, some forms of asthma, rheumatism, ulcers, colds, thyroid malfunction, arthritis, migraine headaches, blindness, and a host of stomach disorders apart from ulcers. It also causes palpitations, pains in the back of the neck, indigestion, nausea, constipation, diarrhea, dizziness, unexplainable fatigue, insomnia, allergies, and temporary paralysis.

Many other reasons could be given to substantiate the fact that worry is a sin.

Worry is a sin because it is symptomatic of prayerlessness.

> Moreover as for me, God forbid that I should sin against the Lord in ceasing to pray for you . . . (1 Samuel 12:23).

No one can pray and worry at the same time.

> Thou wilt keep him in perfect peace, whose mind is stayed on thee: because he trusteth in thee (Isaiah 26:3).

When you pray your mind is staid on Christ and you have His assurance of perfect peace. Worry is therefore banished.

Worry is a sin because of what it does to family life.

> Wives, submit yourselves unto your own husbands, as unto the Lord.
>
> Husbands, love your wives, even as Christ also loved the church, and gave himself for it.
>
> Nevertheless let every one of you in particular so love his wife even as himself; and the wife see that she reverence her husband (Ephesians 5:22,25,33).

These injunctions in the book of Ephesians are violated and disobeyed when worry is in the saddle.

Worry is a sin because it undermines our Christian witness. In Matthew 5:16 Jesus says:

> Let your light so shine before men, that they may see your good works, and glorify your Father which is in heaven.

Someone may say, "Oh, yes, Mr. Haggai, you can talk like that in an overly confident, pedantic manner. You are young and enjoy good health, but you don't know what I have to put up with."

Let me say, friend, that I too hold the distinction of having suffered a "nervous breakdown." The reason I put the words "nervous breakdown" in quotes is that most so-called nervous breakdowns do not originate with any organic problem in the nervous system. Actually, most of what goes under the label "nervousness" ought to be called mental maladjustment.

When I was 24 years old and pastor of my first church, I suffered one of those so-called "nervous breakdowns" which was but the culmination of stress, anxiety, and worry. I was full-time pastor of a church, taking 19 college hours, and conducting evangelistic campaigns. My wife felt sorry for me. My church felt sorry for me. My doctor felt sorry for me. But no one felt as sorry for me as I felt for myself. Finally the doctor ordered me to get away for several weeks of rest and diversion. My church graciously made this possible.

During those weeks of convalescence God spoke to my heart and showed me that my condition was not the result of any organic difficulty, but the result of the *sin* of worry. With gratitude to God I can say that since the fall of 1948 I have not lost five minutes of sleep over any problem, difficulty, tension, worry, or any adverse circumstance of life whatsoever. Today my physical condition is as perfect as can be. In fact, an insurance company returned to me the culmination of seven years of penalties I had been paying on premiums because of a condition in my 20's which they feared. I attribute the improved physical condition to the conquest of worry.

Worry is a sin. The Bible is the only book that deals adequately with the problem of sin. Quite logically, then, we go to the Word of God to find the solution to this problem.

> Rejoice in the Lord alway: and again I say, Rejoice.
> Let your moderation be known unto all men. The Lord is at hand.

> Be careful for nothing; but in every thing by prayer and supplication with thanksgiving let your requests be made known unto God.
>
> And the peace of God, which passeth all understanding, shall keep your hearts and minds through Christ Jesus.
>
> Finally, brethren, whatsoever things are true, whatsoever things are honest, whatsoever things are just, whatsoever things are pure, whatsoever things are lovely, whatsoever things are of good report; if there be any virtue, and if there be any praise, think on these things (Philippians 4:4-8).

> Delight yourselves in the Lord, yes, find your joy in him at all times. Have a reputation for gentleness, and never forget the nearness of your Lord.
>
> Don't worry over anything whatever; tell God every detail of your needs in earnest and thankful prayer, and the peace of God, which transcends human understanding, will keep constant guard over your hearts and minds as they rest in Christ Jesus.
>
> My brothers I need only add this. If you believe in goodness and if you value the approval of God, fix your minds on whatever is true and honourable and just and pure and lovely and admirable (Philippians 4:4-8—Phillips).

Now give thought to the words of our Lord in Matthew 6:25-34:

> Therefore I tell you, stop being perpetually uneasy (anxious and worried) about your life, what you shall eat or what you shall drink, and about your body, what you shall put on. Is not life greater (in quality) than food, and the body (far above and more excellent) than clothing? Look at the birds of the air; they neither sow nor reap nor gather into barns, and yet your heavenly Father keeps feeding them. Are you not worth more than they? And

which of you by worrying and being anxious can add one unit of measure (cubit) to his stature or to the span of his life? (Psalm 39:5-7). And why should you be anxious about clothes? Consider the lilies of the field and learn thoroughly how they grow; they neither toil nor spin; Yet I tell you, even Solomon in all his magnificence (excellence, dignity and grace) was not arrayed like one of these (1 Kings 10:4-7). But if God so clothes the grass of the field, which today is alive and green and tomorrow is tossed into the furnace, will He not much more surely clothe you, O you men with little faith?

Therefore do not worry and be anxious, saying, What are we going to have to eat? or, What are we going to have to drink? or, What are we going to have to wear? For the Gentiles (heathen) wish for and crave and diligently seek after all these things; and your heavenly Father well knows that you need them all. But seek for (aim at and strive after) first of all His kingdom, and His righteousness (His way of doing and being right), and then all these things taken together will be given you besides.

So do not worry or be anxious about tomorrow, for tomorrow will have worries and anxieties of its own. Sufficient for each day is its own trouble (Matthew 6:25-34—*Amplified New Testament*).

The passage in Philippians 4:4-8 constitutes the biblical basis for this book. Out of these verses the thesis of this book is lifted. As we progress, other Scriptures will be used to give added emphasis, insights, illustrations.

Now here is the formula for victory over worry:

Praise plus **Poise** plus **Prayer** equals **Peace**.

Subsequent chapters will amplify and develop this formula found in Philippians 4. The factors involved in praise and in poise and in prayer will be discussed. Suggestions—specific suggestions—will be made for the purpose of assisting you in putting this formula into practice.

Observance of this formula would sweeten the atmosphere of many homes, convert many a faltering business into a thriving success, significantly improve the scholastic level of many a student, give meaning and purpose to many an aimless life, and deliver many a person from a premature grave by curing what is now psychosomatic illness (that is, a physical disorder orginating in or aggravated by emotional turbulence) but which would, if left alone, deteriorate into organic illness.

Remember the formula: **Praise** plus **Poise** plus **Prayer** equals **Peace**. Write this formula in large letters. Place one on the mirror of your medicine cabinet where you shave or on the mirror of your dresser. It will be well for the husband to place one in a conspicuous place in the office where he works and for the housewife to have one placed over the sink or in some prominent place where it will catch her eye during the daytime. It will also be well if you will attach one to the sun visor in your automobile. You will find great profit if you will place this formula in several conspicuous places where it will command your attention several times during the day.

Let me further suggest that you memorize the verses found in Philippians 4:4-8. It will be helpful for you to repeat them aloud every morning and every night until they become a part of you.

Now you are ready to begin the discussion of the cure of this vicious sin, worry.

Part 2

PRAISE

4

The Requirement to Rejoice

Rejoice evermore (1 Thessalonians 5:16).

Rejoice in the Lord alway: and again I say, Rejoice (Philippians 4:4).

Delight yourselves in the Lord, yes, find your joy in him at all times (Philippians 4:4—Phillips).

You say, "But I don't feel like rejoicing. I don't feel like being happy." By that you mean that the circumstances engulfing you are not such as contribute to your happiness.

The majority of people who are chronic worriers make the ridiculous mistake of waiting until the circumstances engulfing them change. You must change the circumstances whenever possible, but happiness is not a state of becoming, it is a state of being. You don't acquire happiness. You assume happiness.

Notice that the verse (Philippians 4:4) is in the imperative mood. It is mandatory. Paul doesn't say, "If you are so disposed let me suggest that you rejoice." No. He says, "Rejoice in the Lord alway: and again I say, Rejoice." Literally it could be translated, "Keep on rejoicing in the Lord always: and again I say, keep on rejoicing." Make the joy of the Lord the habit pattern of your life. When you fail to do this, you sin.

You rejoice when you praise. You cannot praise God without rejoicing in God and rejoicing in the circumstances, no matter how unpleasant, which God permits.

The word *praise* in its various forms, and the word *rejoice* in its various forms, are mentioned more than 550 times in the Word of God. The very fact that this subject receives such repetitious attention in the Book of God indicates its importance.

In Psalm 34:1 David said:

> I will bless the Lord at all times: his praise shall continually be in my mouth.

Praise was the habit pattern of David's life even though, like you, David had many troubles and difficulties. He often passed through deep waters. One son, Adonijah, broke his heart. Absalom, another son, betrayed his father and tried to usurp his authority. Another son, Amnon, brought grief to David's heart when he committed adultery with his half sister, Tamar. You also remember how viciously Shimei cursed David on one occasion. Every Sunday school pupil remembers the story of Saul's persecution of David. Saul repeatedly sought David's life and with barbaric treachery hounded him. Yet in all of this David blessed the Lord and fulfilled the requirement to rejoice. God's praise was continually in David's mouth.

In Psalm 33:1 David admonishes us to:

> Rejoice in the Lord, O ye righteous: for praise is comely for the upright.

This is the injunction of the man who was "a man after God's own heart."

After Peter and the apostles had been beaten mercilessly for speaking "in the name of Jesus," they departed, "rejoicing that they were counted worthy to suffer shame for His name" (Acts 5:41).

You are entitled to no particular commendation simply because you rejoice when everything goes well. When, however, you have made praise and rejoicing the habit pattern of your life, you have arrived at that place where you not only bring glory to God, but you set up an immunity against worry.

Rejoice even on blue Mondays and black Fridays.

Though it seems that friends have betrayed you, neighbors are vicious and mean to you, relatives don't appreciate you, and tragedy overtakes you, you will conquer worry with the attitude expressed in Isaiah 12:2,4:

> Behold, God is my salvation; I will trust, and not be afraid: for the Lord Jᴇʜᴏᴠᴀʜ is my strength and my song; he also is become my salvation.
> And in that day shall ye say, Praise the Lord, call upon his name, declare his doings among the people, make mention that his name is exalted.

The late Mr. Owen Cooper of Yazoo City, Mississippi, is one of the nation's outstanding Christian laymen and one of Mississippi's top-ranking citizens. Sometime ago his beautiful home, representing the dreams and hard work of many years, went up in smoke. Some of the members of the family barely escaped with their lives. The fire completely gutted the home and destroyed nearly everything of value.

Shortly after the terrible fire, Mr. Cooper's pastor, Dr. Harold Shirley, told me that the entire family was in prayer meeting the following night. In that service Mr. Cooper arose during the testimony time and with a radiance that only God can give expressed his gratitude to the Lord for sparing their lives. He had learned years before the truth of Romans 8:28:

> And we know that all things work together for good to them that love God, to them who are the called according to his purpose.

Despite this calamity, the habit pattern of the Cooper family could not be affected adversely.

Remember what has been said previously. There is no condition or circumstance that can justify worry. Worry is a sin. Praise is an antidote to worry.

One of the most radiant Christian men I have ever met passed through a heart-crushing trial several years ago. To help augment the family income during the depression, he and his wife provided room and board for a "highly respected citizen." The man whom they took in turned out to be a Judas, a betrayer. He seduced my friend's wife with diabolical cunning. When she tried to break off the relationship he went berserk. He strangled her and then put her baby in the oven and turned on the gas, murdering the little one by asphyxiation. He then took the couple's eight-year-old son out into the garage and strangled him with a piece of wire. Then the depraved man returned to the kitchen, lay down on some chairs in front of the stove, with all the gas jets on.

The rescue squad was able to revive the viperous murderer. But my friend lost his wife and children in that one terrible series of tragedies.

This crushing blow would have upset the mental balance of a lesser man than my radiant Christian friend. In the strength of the Lord he actually went to the penitentiary to witness to the murderer of his entire family. The way my friend conducted himself through that ordeal and during the subsequent years has had an impact for good and for God that words cannot express. Of course he was grief-stricken. But through it all the joy of the Lord remained his abiding and unwavering possession.

You say you have troubles? Surely you do. We all have. When rejoicing has become the habit pattern of your life you are not a thermometer personality registering the temperature of your environment. You are rather a thermostat personality setting the temperature. You have learned, in the words of Paul to "Rejoice evermore" (1 Thessalonians 5:16).

Paul was no "ivory tower theorist." He urged the Christians at Philippi to "Rejoice in the Lord alway: and again I say, Rejoice" (Philippians 4:4). He was a prisoner in Rome. He did not say, "Cry with me," or "Mourn with me," but "Rejoice with me." What a hysterical time he could have had, waiting to be martyred. If he could rejoice in an hour like that, what excuse can we find for our anxieties?

To help you obey this commandment—obedience to which will revolutionize your life—let me suggest some helps.

5

How to Control Your F

Think and act joyfully and you will feel joyful. You can control your feelings by controlling your thoughts and your actions.

It is a basic law of human nature that you will feel as you act or think. In other words, if you don't feel the way you want to feel, think and act the way you ought to feel, and soon you will feel the way you are thinking and acting—ideally this will be the way God wants you to feel. I will give you an illustration. Go to a quiet room, stand with your feet about a foot apart at the heels and at 45-degree angles. Clasp your hands behind your back, letting them hang loosely. Bow your back and neck and head slightly, maintaining complete relaxation of the body. Now start thinking resentful thoughts.

Did you observe what happened? Immediately you straightened up because of the contraction of your muscles. You became taut. Your thoughts, actions, and feelings are interrelated.

When a man comes into my study and sits down in a relaxed manner, placing the ankle of his right leg loosely over the knee of his left leg and leans back, I know he has absolute confidence in me. He has no fear of me, for a position of defense would be hard to assume from this posture.

Carry this over into your everyday life. When you are depressed and forlorn and feel that you have nothing but trouble, *smile. Throw your shoulders back. Take a good deep breath. Sing.* Better still, *force yourself to laugh.* Keep forcing it until you are laughing heartily. At first it will seem mockery, but I guarantee you, it will chase away your gloom.

You cannot think *fear* and act *courageously*. Conversely, you cannot think *courage* and act *fearfully*. You cannot think *hatred* and act *kindly*. Conversely, you cannot think *kindly* and act

43

atefully. Your feelings inevitably correspond to your dominant thoughts and actions.

Is this scriptural? Absolutely! God's Word says, "For as he thinketh in his heart so is he" (Proverbs 23:7).

Now once again read verse eight of our text and see how important it is.

> Finally, brethren, whatsoever things are true, whatsoever things are honest, whatsoever things are just, whatsoever things are pure, whatsoever things are lovely, whatsoever things are of good report; if there be any virtue, and if there be any praise, think on these things (Philippians 4:8).

Obedience to the command of verse eight will result in obedience to the command of verse four. As you think, so will you feel. Our feelings are revealed by our actions. For instance, when I see a man with his feet set at ten minutes to two and his lips at 20 past eight, who pushes his weight instead of carrying it, I say to myself, "Watch out. This man is a potential tyrant." When I see a woman nervously moving her wedding band back and forth on her ring finger, I often assume she is suffering from the itch—or more probably she and her husband are not getting along too well.

No, you may not be able to directly control your feelings, but you can control your thoughts and actions voluntarily. Therefore, in the strength of Christ, master your thoughts and actions and thus dominate your feelings.

It is impossible for you to "rejoice in the Lord always" and to worry at the same time. Furthermore, you cannot remove worry thoughts and fear thoughts by simply saying, "I don't want to be afraid. I don't want to worry."

If you would win over worry, discipline yourself to think upon the "these things" of verse eight. Chapter 10 will give added insight on this subject. Let your actions accommodate themselves to your thoughts. Discipline yourself to smile, to maintain good posture, to talk with a musical voice in a dynamic manner—in short, to act in a manner compatible with these positive thoughts.

Don't start tomorrow; start *today*. Start *now*. Your worries will flee. God will be glorified.

Mr. Robert E. (Bob) Glaze of Dallas, Texas, has distinguished himself as a Bible teacher, a patron of the arts, a civic leader, a family man, and a businessman.

He is a member of the President's Council of the Dallas Symphony Association. He has taught a Bible class every Sunday morning for 40 years or more, and he has been written up in such prestigious business publications as *Fortune* as an outstanding businessman.

Bob is a certified public accountant by profession. Things went very well for him from the time he was discharged from the Navy where he served as an officer during World War II. After several years as a comptroller for a large organization, he and three friends decided to go into business for themselves. The business collapsed within a year. Bob did not panic, did not go into the trough of depression, but he took control of his situation and, like a superb sea captain, skillfully maneuvered the ship of his life through dangerous and uncharted waters.

He would not compromise with just any position that came along. He determined what he would like to do and with whom he would like to be associated. His number-one choice was America's leading developer, Mr. Trammel Crow of Dallas.

Bob had heard that Trammel Crow was a fitness buff. So Bob got into first-class shape himself. He was 43 years old at the time. He made an appointment with Trammel Crow. During the interview, Trammel suggested they visit the fourteenth floor of one of his buildings. Bob had heard that Trammel did not take elevators but, rather, ran up the steps. When Trammel arrived at the fourteenth floor, Bob was right behind him. Later Bob chuckled as he recounted the experience and said, "I don't know if Trammel hired me because he thought I was a good man for the job or because he was impressed that I could stay with him up the 14 flights of stairs!"

The point I'm making is that Bob kept his focus so tightly on his objective that he did not permit a divided mind. He gave no room to worry at all. He controlled his feelings by controlling his thoughts and his actions.

And he secured the position he wanted to the delight of both Mr. Crow and himself.

In November 1986, Bob was rushed to the hospital with a severe case of pancreatitis. His sickness and the complications from it lasted for more than seven months. As I understand it, rogue enzymes were attacking vital organs and endangering his life. The cause of the problem was a bad gall bladder situation. However, Bob was so weak they could not take the chance of operating. For weeks on end, he was fed intravenously. Three times, according to the doctors, they nearly lost him. After his gall bladder surgery, Bob announced to the doctors the day he would go home. They were skeptical, but Bob acted on the conviction that the surgery was a success and that he would be home earlier than the doctors had originally suggested . . . and he was.

This is no appeal to foolhardiness. Bob would not be imprudent. He would be positive.

Today, in his late 60's, he is back at his usual pace, which would make the tongue of a vigorous young man hang out.

Bob is quick to acknowledge that God supernaturally intervened in restoring him to health. He and his wife Ruth believe that God heard the prayers of literally thousands of Christian friends around the world. And he is quick to give God the glory, as are all of us who had a share in helping to love him and pray him through this ordeal. However, I must quickly point out that Bob, during this time, never permitted himself to focus his attention on anything except the expectation that he would survive, get well, and live a vigorous and fruitful life.

I submit to you that God honored his faith and the faith of his friends—and God also honored the focus of his mind, which gave foundation to the kind of emotions that are helpful in healing.

If you have not read *Anatomy of an Illness* by Norman Cousins, I suggest you do it. Norman Cousins, the famous writer and editor, was not expected to live. He concluded that if bad emotions can induce illness, why should not good emotions contribute to health?

I'm not making an appeal for an empty-headed assault on reality. I am making an appeal for reality.

Did not the sage say, "A merry heart doeth good like a medicine"?

Norman Cousins controlled his emotions by controlling his thoughts. That's exactly what Bob Glaze did. Norman Cousins has lived a productive life for more than a decade after the doctor said he could not survive. And Bob Glaze came through his ordeal very recently, at the time of this writing there is every evidence to believe that God has great things yet for him to achieve—and by God's grace, he'll do it. He controls his feelings by controlling his thoughts and his actions.

Much damage is done to the cause of Christ by professing Christians who shout out their defeatism and negativism by the limp manner with which they shake hands, the listless way in which they walk, the sourpuss countenance they maintain, and the plaintive and whining way in which they speak. I believe that these people do more damage to the cause of Christ than all of the bootleggers, extortionists, whoremongers, drunkards, and the riffraff of society's gutter put together.

Several years ago as pastor of a large church in a Southern city, I faced problems that would have challenged my sanity had it not been for the grace of God. Though it was kept from the congregation, several of the leaders and I learned that one of the senior deacons was enmeshed in sin. To make matters worse, he showed no signs of remorse and evidenced no desire to repent. Evidence was also uncovered indicating that another prominent member was stealing over $100 a week from the Sunday school offerings. The pressure was on. The question was, "What shall we do? Shall it be made public? If it is made public, will not the testimony of Christ suffer irreparably? Will not the witness for God be hampered irremediably for years to come?"

In addition to these problems, my wife and I had a sorrow in our home. Our precious little son was totally paralyzed. He suffered from cerebral palsy as a result of birth injuries caused by an intoxicated doctor who has since committed suicide. The little fellow was hovering between life and death. Where was the answer to my despondency?

My mind was drawn to Psalm 1. As never before I learned to appreciate the wisdom of that blessed man who delights in the law of the Lord *day and night*. I did not want to feel as I was feeling. It was not a good testimony. Therefore, by God's grace I fastened my thoughts upon the "these things" of Philippians 4:8 and endeavored to act in a compatible manner. On several occasions I would get into my car, drive outside the city, and literally force myself to laugh and to sing. I'm sure some passersby thought I was crazy. But this procedure was what kept me from going crazy!

Think and act the way God would have you to think and act. Result? You will feel as you think and act. This will glorify God. It will help you give worry the brush-off.

6

Count Your Many Blessings

If you would utilize this tonic of praise as an antidote to worry, you must *count your many blessings.*

Here again you must "gird up the loins of your mind" and with sheer determined effort force yourself, if necessary, to focus your attention upon all of the blessings God has so lavishly bestowed upon you. Read the Psalms for help in this.

Your blessings may not be material blessings, but they are real blessings, nevertheless. Actually, no man has ever found joy simply because he acquired material gain. Joy does not consist in the abundance of our material possessions.

> . . . for a man's life consisteth not in the abundance of the things which he possesseth (Luke 12:15b).

For how much money would you sell the health that God has given to you? How much does your wife's love mean to you? Have you ever thoroughly evaluated the value of your child's devotion? For what amount would you sell your reputation if it could be put on the open market? What premium do you put upon the eyesight God has given you—and the capacity to hear, and to speak, and to feel, and to taste? Have you ever thought how impoverished you would be if suddenly you were to be deprived of all your friends?

We tend to take the manifold blessings of God for granted, don't we? Start counting your blessings; your heart will overflow with gratitude and your lips with praise.

You may have heard the following story:

> There was a king who was so unhappy that he dispatched one of his men to go on a trip and find a

happy man. The king ordered, "When you find the happy man, purchase his shirt and bring it back to me that I might wear it and also be happy." For years the king's man traveled and searched. He could not find a happy man. Finally, one day when he was walking in one of the poorer sections of one of the most impoverished countries he heard a man singing at the top of his voice. He followed the sound and found a man who was plowing a field. He asked the plowman, "Are you happy?"

The plowman replied, "I have never known a day of unhappiness."

The king's representative then told the plowman the purpose of his mission.

The plowman laughed uproariously as he replied, "Why, man, I don't have a shirt!"

Also speaking of gratitude are the following lines:

"I had the blues because I had no shoes

Until upon the street I met a man who had no feet."

Count your blessings. If it will help you, periodically take a piece of paper and write out your blessings. Praise God for the love of your wife, the affection of your children, your good health, the encouragement of your friends. As you exert some effort along this line, blessings by the score will come crowding into your consciousness and you will jump to your feet, your heart singing, "Praise God from whom all blessings flow!" And you will be honoring the Lord in obeying the exhortation of Philippians 4:4.

How precious also are thy thoughts unto me, O God! how great is the sum of them!

If I should count them, they are more in number than the sand: when I awake, I am still with thee (Psalm 139:17,18).

> Many, O Lord my God, are thy wonderful works
> which thou hast done, and thy thoughts which are
> to us-ward: they cannot be reckoned up in order
> unto thee: if I would declare and speak of them,
> they are more than can be numbered (Psalm 40:5).

Spurgeon, the great Baptist preacher of the last century, wrote of a young man who had suffered an accident in which he had broken his hip. The hip did not heal properly and it left the man crippled. Earnestly the people prayed that God would restore this young man to health and strength. Shortly after the people began their intense and concerted intercession on behalf of this young man, apparent tragedy struck—the young man fell and broke his hip again. Was his a tragedy? It would have been completely natural for him and for the intercessors to begin to complain, for it seemed as though the condition was much worse. Fortunately many of the intercessors—wise and mature Christians—saw God's hand in the entire affair. They began praising Him and thanking Him for the blessing. Now the hip was set properly. It wasn't long until convalescence under God's leadership had done its perfect work. The young man walked with no limp whatsoever. The tragedy was a blessing.

Count your blessings! Even when things seem to go wrong, thank God and take courage. Say with the apostle Paul:

> Most gladly, therefore, will I rather glory in my
> infirmities that the power of Christ may rest upon
> me (2 Corinthians 12:9b).

In 1950 the Lord blessed us with a precious baby boy. Due to a tragedy described in detail a little later in this book, the little fellow nearly died. God was pleased to spare him, but he was now totally paralyzed. He had a keen mind and normal inclinations and desires, but his body would not respond to the demands of his will. Oh, yes, it hurt—hurt him and hurt us. However, God gave him a marvelously sweet disposition.

Was his paralysis and condition as a cerebral palsy victim a blessing? Yes. *Definitely so.* Between the year of his birth and the year I resigned the pastorate to go into full-time evangelism I undoubtedly buried more little babies and small children and ministered to more sick children than any man in any pastorate. God had conditioned me in a special way for a peculiar and yet a blessed ministry that He was about to entrust to me. The life of my son was a distinct blessing. There are many ways in which I could demonstrate this, but they involve experiences locked up in the cherished and secret places of my heart and open only to God and our immediate family.

Johnny died in 1975, 16 years after the first edition of *How To Win Over Worry*. People came from as far as 5000 miles away to his funeral. One man who drove from a distant city said, "I never knew exactly how to express to Johnny what an inspiration he was to me. I wanted to come here, because I'm sure he's conscious of this service, and I just want him to know how much he meant to me."

Letters from every continent on earth poured in after his death—people telling what a blessing his life had been to them.

Christine, my wife, always looked upon Johnny's life as a special blessing from the Lord. That attitude takes the sting out of hurt and the power out of worry.

In one of the prominent nations in the news, an Asian nation, a young minister of the gospel preaches to between 1200 and 1500 people every Sunday. In that nation people have been slaughtered by the thousands. When I met with this remarkable leader in a neutral capital of the world, I said, "How do you handle the pressure of trying to maintain a ministry in a city and nation vocally committed to the destruction of Christianity?"

He smiled at me and said, "How good is God. What blessings He bestows!" I thought to myself, "This poor fellow didn't hear what I said." But then the minister went on to explain.

"God has put us in the eye of the storm. On one side are the Communists. On the other side are the Muslims. They are in such hostile combat with each other that by being in the center we are wonderfully protected. Better still, hundreds are coming to know Christ as Savior."

This man was not bemoaning his lot; he was counting his blessings. I don't think that worry finds him a suitable host.

During my visits to Vietnam in the late '60's and early '70's, I met with many Vietnamese people. One man stands out. He told me how he regretted the war, how sorry he was that it was necessary for American boys to come and suffer separation from home, injury, and even death. Then he said, "The greatest victory of this conflict is that the Americans and the Koreans brought the gospel to our village, and we who were in darkness came to know Jesus Christ." This man had lost members of his family. He had lost his business. His home had been burned to the ground. He knew how to count his blessings!

During the Korean conflict, 1950-53, Presbyterian missionary Dr. Harold Voekel had a penetrating and pervasive ministry among the troops—on both sides. He personally won to faith in Christ more than 150 North Korean soldiers, 20 of whom are now in the full-time gospel ministry.

It was Voekel who introduced my mother and father, so I have more than a casual appreciation for that gentleman. The characteristic that captured my attention every time I was with Dr. Voekel was his bouyant and resilient Christian optimism in any situation. He knew how to count his blessings, and worry never seemed to quite catch up with him.

"Count your blessings. Name them one by one, and it will surprise you what the Lord has done." And one of the greatest surprises will be the fact that you are no longer saddled by that monster, worry, who has been riding herd on you.

Let me urge again that when you become depressed and worried, take a piece of paper and literally force yourself to write out in detail every blessing that comes to mind. Concentrate. Think hard. Surely it will take time, but not as much time as worrying will. It won't take as much time as an interview at the psychiatrist's office and it will be considerably cheaper. Furthermore, in the strength of God you will be actively doing something about your own condition. This is much more effective than passively responding to psychotherapy.*

In chapter 7 consideration is given to a most important factor in the matter of praise.

---

*Please do not miscontrue what has been written as an expression of disregard for the effectiveness of all professional counseling and for its importance in certain situations. Nevertheless, there are many people who today are frequenting the offices of psychiatrists who could be enjoying mental and emotional health had they only taken certain precautions and observed the biblical formula—**Praise** plus **Poise** plus **Prayer** equals **Peace**—earlier in their life.

7

Anticipate Apathy

Don't expect to be appreciated. When you are appreciated it will be like the cherry on top of the whipped cream of your strawberry sundae—something a little special.

Let not your rejoicing be dependent upon appreciation shown to you.

Our Lord healed ten lepers. Do you remember how many came back to thank Him? That's right. One!

The late General Harry C. Trexler, a wealthy philanthropist and outstanding citizen of Allentown, Pennsylvania, was providing the financial needs for 40 college students in 1933, the year in which he died. Four months before his death he called his secretary in and inquired how many young men and women he was sending through college. She told him. With mixed bewilderment and grief he replied, "And last Christmas I got only one or two Christmas cards from this group."

Many times, when discussing this prevalent ingratitude, I have stated in a jocular vein, "Would you believe it? Why there are some people who don't even appreciate me!"

Expect ingratitude. Give for the joy of giving and soon you will be so thrillingly occupied with this privilege of giving that you will not have time to reflect upon the ingratitude of others.

Sometime ago I read about a man in New York who, over a period of more than four decades, helped more than 5000 young people secure positions in New York City. When discussing it sometime later he observed that only six had expressed gratitude.

Years ago there was a shipwreck in Lake Michigan. A powerful swimmer who was then a student at Northwestern University rescued 23 persons before he finally collapsed.

Some years after that, in Los Angeles, Dr. R. A. Torrey was telling the story about this young man's concern and his heroic deeds. To his astonishment he found out that the man, now old, was in the audience. In talking with the rescuer, he asked him what was the most significant thing about the rescue—the thing that stood out most in his memory after all the intervening years. The rescuer dropped his eyes and in a low voice said, "Not a one said 'thanks.' "

Have you ever read about Aristotle's ideal man? Here is the philosopher's definition of the ideal man. "The ideal man takes joy in doing favors for others; but he feels ashamed to have others do favors for him. For it is a mark of superiority to confer a kindness; but it is a mark of inferiority to receive it."

Paul reminded the Christians to whom he was speaking that "It is more blessed to give than to receive" (Acts 20:35). Therefore, let your joy arise out of the blessedness of giving, of helping, of doing. Not expecting gratitude, find your joy in the very act of service.

Years ago Samuel Johnson said, "Gratitude is a fruit of great cultivation. You do not find it among gross people."

I am sure you have noticed how many times when friends move away from us or we change residence to a distant city, how eloquent and emotional we are in affirming that we will stay in touch—we'll write letters, we'll phone, we'll visit. Think back and ask yourself how often such resolutions have been carried out, whether it was with your gang at the college dormitory, your buddies in the military service, your neighbors down the street, the friends you met on a 60-day cruise overseas, your coworkers at the office or factory, or whatever.

It's not that we intend to ignore our friends. It's the apathy within us that does the work. Unless you, yourself, take measures to counteract the apathy natural to all of us, you'll lose the benefit of continuing relationships and uplifting experiences. But when you have examined your own heart, you'll not find it so difficult to grasp why others are also apathetic.

Take the matter of class reunions. Usually there are one or two spark plugs in the class. Were it not for them, there would be no reunions. They are the ones that take action, aggressively contact all the other members, and take steps to bring about a completely delightful experience of getting together after years of absence from each other.

It was the sage who said, "He who would have friends must show himself friendly." And maintaining friendships takes discipline, time, and energy.

To the degree that you understand the natural inclination toward apathy in your own life and grasp the insight regarding those whom you feel should not be apathetic to you—to that degree you will increase your capacity for the component of praise, the deterrent to worry and its divided mind.

It is quite evident as you read the Pauline epistles that some of the very people whom Paul won to faith in Jesus Christ turned upon him and reviled him maliciously.

Do you know what is the basic sin? Someone answers, "Unbelief." No, if you will read Romans 1:21 you will conclude that ingratitude is at the root of all sin whether that ingratitude be active or whether it be passive:

> Because that, when they knew God, they glorified him not as God, neither were thankful; but became vain in their imaginations, and their foolish heart was darkened (Romans 1:21).

Was not ingratitude the root of the sin committed by Adam and Eve?

Consider it. The Lord Jesus Christ died for us "while we were yet sinners" (Romans 5:8). He suffered. He bled. He died—for *us*. Yet there are millions who, knowing this, refuse to accept Him as Savior and Lord. Why? Ingratitude!

Ingratitude is a universal sin. Expect it. Give for the joy of giving. Do for the joy of doing. Help only for the joy of helping. And you won't have time even to notice the prevalence of the sin of ingratitude.

Praise should be the habit pattern of your life regardless of the cold and even cruel treatment received from some whom you have helped.

8

Master the Art of Altruism

If you would conquer worry with this weapon of *praise* you must master the art of altruism.

Become genuinely interested in other people. Love your neighbor as yourself. Honor God by losing your life in serving others. By "others" I am referring not only to your employer or your family, but also to all those whom God gives you the privilege of serving.

An upset young college man sought counseling from Dr. George W. Truett who was pastor of First Baptist Church of Dallas, Texas at that time. The student had passed through troubled waters. He said he was ready to give up his faith and that he had lost all confidence in God and people. Wisely and patiently Dr. Truett listened to this young man. When the student finished his tale of woe, the wise and patient pastor asked the young man for a favor. The young man agreed. Dr. Truett then gave the young man the name of the hospital and the room number of a patient who was in need of a visit. Said the great-hearted minister, "I just don't have time to make the visit. You make it for me." The young man assented.

He came away from that hospital bed a new man. As a favor to the mighty pastor in Dallas, the young man determined to do his best. He did so well that he became genuinely interested in the patient. In so doing, his own difficulties and despair were dispelled.

Uncle Joe Hawk was one of the most radiant personalities I ever met. For more than half a century he was a member of the First Baptist Church of Cleveland, Tennessee. When I met him, he was 87 years old but younger than many 25-year-old-people. He attended every service I conducted in that good church in 1953.

Let me tell you a little about him and you will catch an insight into his sparkling vitality at 87. Years before, during the depression, the First Baptist Church of Cleveland, Tennessee was in straitened circumstances. Uncle Joe Hawk was a drayman. He had been blessed with a good business, but of course he was suffering as were the other businessmen during those oppressive years. Nevertheless, he forgot himself. This dear man lost himself in his concern for that church and its people, many of whom had not yet accepted Christ.

At the risk of putting a calamitous crimp in his business, Uncle Joe sold his two finest dray horses. He gave the money to the church. Because of his gift the First Baptist Church of Cleveland, Tennessee, stands as a mighty citadel for Christ today. Few people knew what he did. He did it without fanfare. In fact, many of the church members today are unaware of this tremendous sacrifice. Uncle Joe never got the money back from the church. He didn't expect to. He didn't want it. He gave it for the sheer joy of giving. He gave it to the eternal glory of God and for the spiritual profit of man. No man who is that interested in others has time to worry about his own problems.

When was the last time you sacrificed and sent anonymously a gift of $50 over and above your tithe to a college or seminary student who was having a hard time? When was the last time you gave something to someone anonymously— a gesture that could in no way profit you from a material standpoint?

Perhaps the mother next door is sick and in great need of help. Why not offer to take care of the children for a couple of days? True, they may be little monsters. That is all the more reason your help would be a great benefit to their mother. When your neighbor goes on vacation, why not offer to take care of the mail and send it on? Why not drop a line of appreciation to that teacher who has taken such an interest in your child and has made such a distinct contribution to his highest good? Drop a line of gratitude to your pastor for the message that was such a blessing to you. Encourage him. It will take only a few moments of time and a stamp.

Does not the Word of God tell us we are to esteem others better than ourselves?

> Let nothing be done through strife or vainglory;
> but in lowliness of mind let each esteem other better
> than themselves (Philippians 2:3).

Let me earnestly suggest that you determine to do something specific for someone every day—something for which no remuneration of any kind will be sought or expected. You may exclaim, "Shades of the Boy Scouts!" but this is what good religion is all about and besides, it will relieve you of that time you normally give to worrying. Your cup will run over with the joy of the Lord.

Go ahead, do it *now*. If it doesn't come to you easily and if you don't know how to begin, simply sit down and ask the Lord to guide you. With pencil and paper write down some things that come to your mind.

Perhaps the Lord will lead you to do the washing for the lady next door who has been hampered by her day-and-night care of sick children. Perhaps you will contact the head of some fine Christian college or one of our seminaries to secure the name of a student who is in great need. You will help him. You may be led to invite a serviceman to have dinner with you on Sunday (we are not as thoughtful along that line as we were during the war years). There is no point in my going on; you take it from here.

I am persuaded that my mother, who suffered major illnesses for the last 45 years of her life—she died at 80—lived such a long and fruitful life because of the way she immersed herself in serving others. When a family moved into the neighborhood, she would be there with some warm food while they were getting settled. When someone was sick, she would take a card to them, as well as some thoughtful little present. She maintained correspondence with hundreds of people around the world.

I think that serving others created in her a greater capacity to praise. She was a mild-mannered lady, quiet of demeanor, but a person of strong will and great capacity to care for others.

To this day, nearly a decade after her final illness and death, people all over the world will talk to me about her. They will tell me some little act of kindness that she had shown toward them. They will produce a postcard, a letter, or a greeting card that she had mailed to them.

One of her close friends died in 1939 in Massachusetts. Mother maintained contact with the four daughters, their spouses, and the grandchildren from 1945, when she left Massachusetts, until late 1978 when she became bedridden.

It is giving, not getting, that induces praise. It is serving, not being served, that develops the highest type of rejoicing. And, of course, no one can rejoice and worry at the same time. The two are mutually exclusive.

If you want to find real joy in living and a genuine escape from worrying, get involved in helping others. It will leave you no time to worry.

A friend of mine, Elmer G. Leterman, visited Honolulu in 1935. In those days, the main mode of travel from the West Coast of mainland United States to Hawaii was by ship. When Leterman descended the gangplank and was greeted effusively by friends who put leis around his neck and his wife's neck, he noticed there were hundreds of people disembarking whom nobody met. They were not given leis. He had hardly unpacked his suitcase at the hotel until he determined that as long as he was in Hawaii, he would meet every boat with a sufficient number of leis to welcome every person who did not have someone meeting him, and put a lei around his neck with the robust "aloha" for which Hawaiian hospitality is internationally known.

As it turned out, people whom he contacted in this way gave him multiplied millions of dollars of business over the next 40 years, even though he didn't show personal interest in people for that purpose. Elmer was a happy man, always upbeat. He had mastered the art of altruism. And it left no room for a divided mind.

Mr. Ee Peng Liang of Singapore is a man past retirement age who has earned the respect not only of the Singapore people, but of people around the world who have watched his humanitarian efforts over the years. He is a chartered accountant by profession and heads up a substantial business in Singapore. The man never ceases to amaze me in his capacity for remembering detail. I met him once. Periodically I will get a note from him with a warm greeting. There is absolutely nothing that I could do for him in a business or personal way except give him the assurance of the continuity of my friendship and respect. But Mr. Ee does not do what he does in order to get. He has mastered the art of altruism, and he impresses me as being one of the most worry-free men I have met in the course of my travels. He has a focused, integrated mind—not a divided mind.

I first heard of Mr. Ee through Mr. Fred Lang, who was for years the head of Dallas Community Chest. Whenever I've visited civic leaders in the Orient, I've been impressed by the numbers who know Mr. Ee and marvel at the contribution he has made to their understanding of the opportunities to help meet the real needs of people.

By all means, use common sense in your efforts to assist other people. Don't be like a certain young Cub Scout who had his own ideas on the subject. One night during a pack meeting the scoutmaster asked all those who had done their good deed for the day to lift their hands. All hands were lifted except the hand of one scout.

The scoutmaster barked out, "Johnny, go out and do your good deed for the day and don't come back until you have done it."

Johnny left. He was gone about 20 minutes. He came back. His clothes were in shreds. His hair was disheveled. His face was cut and bleeding.

The scoutmaster said, "Johnny, what have you been doing?"

Johnny replied, "I did my good deed for the day, sir."

"What was that?" asked the scoutmaster.

"I helped an old lady across the street, sir."

"Well," said the scoutmaster, "how did you get in that condition?"

"She didn't want to go," replied Johnny.

Use common sense in your effort to help others. During the darkest part of the depression a needy family was given an expensive pedigreed French poodle. Doubtless there is much good to be said about a French poodle. But the friend who gave the dog would have been much wiser and more helpful if she had taken the same money and purchased needed clothing and food for the family.

Assist the other person at the point of his greatest need. While doing so, remember "It is more blessed to give than to receive" (Acts 20:35).

Your genuine interest in other people will assassinate the monster of worry. Your positive thoughts of concern for others will crowd out the negative fear-producing thoughts of worry.

Reflect once again upon the concern our Lord showed for others. Even while dying, He cried out, "Father, forgive them for they know not what they do." While in the agonizing process of dying upon the cross He showed concern for His mother and made the finest possible preparation for her after His departure.

Man is as selfish as he dares to be. We are selfish by nature. The middle letter of sin is "I." The middle letter of pride is "I." It takes the cross experience to adequately cancel out the "I." Real Christian discipline in the strength of God is required to master the art of altruism, but the rewards are immeasurable—especially as they relate to the altruist.

Without exception the people who are always rejoicing are people who have mastered this art of altruism—people who are genuinely interested in others. This rejoicing chases away gloom and kills worry.

You will "rejoice in the Lord always" as you faithfully fulfill the injunction in Galatians 6:2-4:

Bear ye one another's burdens, and so fulfil the
law of Christ. For if a man think himself to be

something, when he is nothing, he deceiveth himself. But let every man prove his own work, and then shall he have *rejoicing* in himself alone, and not in another.

I share with you these same verses in the *Amplified New Testament:*

Bear (endure, carry) one another's burdens and troublesome moral thoughts, and in this way fulfill and observe perfectly the law of Christ, the Messiah, and complete what is lacking (in your obedience to it). For if any person thinks himself to be somebody (too important to condescend to shoulder another's load), when he is nobody (of superiority except in his own estimation), he deceives and deludes and cheats himself. But let every person carefully scrutinize and examine and test his own conduct and his own work. He can then have the personal satisfaction and joy of doing something commendable (in itself alone) without (resorting to) boastful comparison with his neighbor (Galatians 6:2-4).

Part 3

POISE

9

Our Impelling Motive

Let your moderation be known unto all men. The Lord is at hand (Philippians 4:5).

Have a reputation for gentleness, and never forget the nearness of your Lord (Philippians 4:5—Phillips).

Now listen to the fuller translation of the *Amplified New Testament:*

Let all men know and perceive and recognize your unselfishness—your considerateness, your forbearing spirit. The Lord is near—He is coming soon.

The word translated in the King James "moderation" can also be translated "suitable," "fair," "reasonable," "gentle," "mild," "patient," and "lenient." The word further carries the idea of "congeniality of spirit." After making a thorough study of the word you will inevitably conclude that I have spelled it correctly—poise—for according to Webster the word *poise* means "balance," "stability," "ease," "dignity of manner," etc.

What is the supreme inducement to poise? What is our impelling motive? What is the driving force that pushes us toward this goal? Here it is in a brief and meaningful message: "The Lord is near"! This is a literal translation of the words in the King James, "the Lord is at hand." In fact, the actual translation would be "the Lord near." Three words! No verb was used. It was not needed. It is abrupt to the point of the dramatic. It is a bolt of light.

The awareness of His nearness gives great calm in the storm and stress of life.

As a child, I was small and sickly. I was the prey of every bully on the school playground. One day during holiday time in the summer of 1934, I was in Grand Rapids, Michigan, with my cousin Alex Haddad. I had accompanied him down to Seymour Square to pick up some groceries for his mother. We had nearly returned to their little house on Burton Street when three big fellows in a pickup truck came by and shouted, "Haddad, get yourself and that blankety-blank Hebrew, Wop, Dago cousin of yours out of here before we mop up the gutter with you."

Immmediately I cringed. I thought to myself, "Uh-oh, here comes another beating." Then I looked over at Alex, and my fears subsided; a peaceful calm replaced them. In fact, I started to smile.

That year, Alex was the AAU wrestling champion in the 175-pound division. At 15, he was much a man. His biceps were like cannonballs and his pectoral muscles were like marble slabs.

Strangely, Alex did not answer back. I said, "Alex, you're not going to let them get by with that, are you?"

"Well, John, you know what the Bible says: If they hit you on one cheek, turn the other."

I had never remembered Alex being that spiritual before, but I was in no position to contest his decision! So I kept walking with him toward the house. We went inside the little picket fence, and just as we got to the front door, he handed the other bag of groceries to me and said, "John, take these in to Mom. Tell her I forget something; I'll be right back."

I knew exactly what he had forgotten. I shoved the groceries inside the front door and then trailed him back down to Seymour Square. I knew exactly what he had in mind. He surmised that the insulting roughnecks were on their way to Miller's ice cream parlor. I got to the location just in time to watch Alex knock one of the three fellows out cold, addle a second fellow with another powerful punch, while the third ran away in stark terror.

I pushed back the shoulders of my four-foot-10-inch frame, brushed the palms of my hands together, and said to myself, "Anyone else?"

What had converted me from a terrified little boy to a calm and serene fellow of positive optimism? A simple answer: Alex was near.

Now, moving from the ridiculous to the sublime, I want you to know that the Lord is near. And living in the awareness of that fact brings about a behavioral change that cannot be explained in human terms. It's often the only major difference between a defeated Christian and a victorious Christian.

Fortune may have eluded you. Culture which you have sought so laboriously becomes ever more painfully remote. Professed love has betrayed you. All these may be true. But "the Lord is near"! There is no mockery in that statement. Those few words assure us, and they impel us to observe the mandates set down in Philippians 4:4-8.

This truth gives urgency and charm to the admonition set down by Paul in this fourth chapter of Philippians.

This statement can refer to Christ's nearness to us right now or to His Second Coming. The best interpreters so agree.

John Calvin, Bishop Moule, and Dean Vaughan all prefer the thought of Christ's present nearness. On the other hand, equally great teachers and commentators such as Dean Alford, F. B. Meyer, and Bishop Lightfoot, prefer the interpretation which is eschatological. They believe the emphasis is on the Second Coming of Christ.

Let us take advantage of the insights of both groups of commentators.

The Lord is near *locally.* "Thou art near, O Lord," sang the psalmist (Psalm 119:151a). And the apostle Paul echoes and glorifies the ancient song.

The Lord is near in that He indwells, by the Holy Spirit, the individual Christian. It is "Christ in you" (Colossians 1:27).

Then the Lord is near from the standpoint of His *availability.* The psalmist cried, "The Lord is nigh unto all them that call upon him" (Psalm 145:18). Here again the New Testament echoes the Old Testament. As children of God we have His ear because we have His heart. A distant Lord would depress us and distress us. An unapproachable Savior could not help us. Thank God, Christ is approachable.

> For we have not an high priest which cannot be touched with the feeling of our infirmities; but was in all points tempted like as we are, yet without sin.
> Let us therefore come boldly unto the throne of grace, that we may obtain mercy, and find grace to help in time of need (Hebrews 4:15,16).

In the exigencies and vicissitudes of life the Lord is near. The psalmist anticipated this truth again. He sang, "The Lord is nigh unto all them that are of a broken heart" (Psalm 34:18). Who has not known the distressful mystery of a broken heart! "God is . . . a very present help in trouble" (Psalm 46:1). The consciousness of Christ's availability induces poise.

Then the Lord is at hand *eschatologically.* He is coming again in clouds of heaven with great glory. I believe His coming is sooner than we think. Very real to the early Christians was the return of our Lord. He Himself declared it in no ambiguous terms.

Jesus may come today. In the silence and darkness of midnight His trumpet may sound and His awful glory blaze upon us!

Our love of His appearing is the greatest inducement to obedience of this admonition to poise in Philippians 4:5. Every injunction mentioned in this book—injunctions all rooted in His divine mandate to us—is more easily fulfilled when we are motivated by the continuous consciousness of the possibility that Jesus may come today. "Be ye also ready" (Matthew 24:44).

The return of our Lord viewed as possibly near should make us rich in Christian character. Contemplation of this truth will make us like Him who is our great Exemplar.

Remember the King James translation of Philippians 4:5: "Let your moderation be known unto all men. The Lord is at hand." The preferable translation of the last sentence is, "The Lord is near." The greatest inducement to poise is the consciousness of the nearness of your Lord. This is the greatest impelling motive to that poise that combats worry.

As you live in the consciousness of the nearness of the Lord, you will find strength that will enable you to observe the biblical formula for peace. You will find strength and inclination to observe the factors involved in the matter of praise.

You will find the factors relating to poise much easier to fulfill as you live in the consciousness of the nearness of your Lord. For instance, you will find that your thoughts are thoughts that please Him and therefore positive thoughts that will put worry on the run. As you live in the consciousness of His nearness you will realize a strength, not your own, enabling you to exercise the self-control that leads to poise and banishes worry.

You will also have victory in the matter of relaxation as you live in the consciousness of the nearness of your Lord.

In the matter of scheduling, the consciousness of the Lord's nearness is a great boon. We avail ourselves of His help. We know that "The steps of a good man are ordered by the Lord" (Psalm 37:23).

Living in the consciousness of the nearness of our Lord will dispel the clouds of pessimism and lead us into the sunshine of enthusiasm and optimism. You cannot live in the consciousness of His nearness and go around looking as if you were born in crab-apple time, put up in vinegar, and weaned on a dill pickle. People who act as though they were born in the kickative mood and the objective case are those who live oblivious to the nearness of the Lord.

With respect to every factor mentioned in Part 3 of this book, fulfillment is largely contingent upon your awareness of the nearness of the Lord.

It goes without saying that Part 4—"Prayer"—of this book is meaningless apart from the consciousness of the nearness of the Lord.

To sum up: The Lord is near *locally.* That should remind us that He is watching everything we do. The Lord is at hand with respect to His *availability.* That assures us of the needed resources to fulfill our every responsibility to Him and for Him. The Lord is at hand *eschatologically.* That reminds us He may come at any time. This induces us always to live in a way that would not shame us if He were to burst unexpectedly upon the scene.

In these three words, then—*the Lord near*—lies dynamic truth. These words are the steam of motive power generating attitudes and activities in fulfillment of the divine demands.

10

Poise Through Thought Control

Finally, brethren, whatsoever things are true, whatsoever things are honest, whatsoever things are just, whatsoever things are pure, whatsoever things are lovely, whatsoever things are of good report; if there be any virtue, and if there be any praise, think on these things (Philippians 4:8).

For as he thinketh in his heart, so is he: Eat and drink, saith he to thee; but his heart is not with thee (Proverbs 23:7).

In chapter 5 the truth was set forth that while we cannot control our feelings directly, we can control them indirectly by controlling our thoughts.

You can control your thoughts directly if you so desire. To be sure, it will take some discipline. Arnold Bennett, in his splendid book, *How to Live on Twenty-Four Hours a Day*, challenges the reader to think on any given subject every day for at least 15 minutes without permitting his mind to wander. I challenge you to try it.

Many people can brood for 15 minutes. They can worry for 15 minutes. But very few people can focus their attention on any given, and I might add worthwhile, subject for 15 minutes without permitting their minds to wander.

To repeat a statement previously made in this book, you cannot think fear and act courage. If you want victory over anxiety, you must develop the control of your thoughts which leads to that poise that conquers worry.

The wisest man of history assures us that we are what we think. That is true. In the words of Marcus Aurelius, "A man's life is what his thoughts make of it." Ralph Waldo Emerson states the truth in another way when he says, "A man is what he thinks about all day long." Our dominant thoughts tend to externalize themselves.

It's an old trick, but school children still love to play it. One will go to Billy and say, "Say, you look terrible. Are you feeling well today?" A little later another one will approach him with a similar suggestion. And then a third. And a fourth. Soon the thought of his not being well becomes Billy's dominant thought—and he goes home sick!

In my first pastorate there was a young lady 29 years of age who maintained an expression on her face that looked like the advance agent of a coming cyclone. She *enjoyed* poor health! Her house was a mess and her general appearance looked like an accident going somewhere to happen. She would come out the front door after the church service and I would shake her hand. It was so limp I felt like handing it back to her. I would say, "How are you?" She would then proceed to tell her tale of woe. I was only 22 years old, but I learned one lesson in a hurry. I stopped asking her how she was. When I shook her hand, I *shook* it, believe me! I gave her my finest smile and said, calling her by name, "You look so much better. You must be feeling better." Believe it or not, within a few months she was looking better and apparently feeling better. With the help of some friends I dropped a seed thought into her mind which became a dominant thought and as she thought, so she became.

Paul says to think on the things that are true. Don't think on falsehood. Think on falsehood and pretty soon you will become false. Your heart will condemn you and your worries will increase.

Think on things that are honest, not dishonest. Your thoughts will tend to externalize themselves. If you think honestly, you live honestly. The word here could be translated, "honorable." Think on things that are honorable. Even if it is true, refuse to think about it if it's dishonorable.

Think on things that are pure. The word used here refers to all sorts of purity. As Peter would say, "Gird up the loins of your mind" (1 Peter 1:13a). An impure thought always precedes an impure deed. Keep your thoughts pure and your deeds will be pure. Pure thoughts are incompatible with worry thoughts.

Think on things that are lovely. This word means "winsome and pleasing." As you embrace thoughts that are winsome and pleasing you will bar from entrance thoughts that produce worry and anxiety.

The apostle Paul says, "Think on things of good report." The words *good report* come from two words meaning "fair-speaking." It could also be translated "attractive." Attractive thoughts will also deliver you from worry. Attractive thoughts will deliver you from being a sourpuss.

Paul then said, "If there be any virtue, and if there be any praise, think on these things." The word *virtue* comes from a word *aresko* which means "to please." Here again learn to control your thoughts so they will relate to that which pleases; they will be pleasing thoughts.

Under God, control your thoughts. Some people are miserable because they are indiscriminate with respect to the guests they invite into their minds. They think worry thoughts, fear thoughts, anxiety thoughts. They don't see the glass half full, they always see it half empty. They are not optimistic, they are pessimistic. They pride themselves by sanctimoniously saying, "I expect the worst so that I will never be disappointed." Expect the worst and you will get the worst. Thoughts of the worst dominating your life tend to externalize themselves into your outward actions so that you become the creator of the worst. You therefore create a self-destroying monster.

Do your own thinking. You must guard yourself even against the well-meaning but oftentimes negative influences and damaging advice of relatives and friends. They mean well, but they often do much damage. Don't leave your mind open to the negative influence of other people. Read the biography of any dynamic personality—any achiever—and almost without exception you will discover that discouraging remarks, poor advice, negative influences, and downright opposition were thrown across his path by the people who were the closest to him.

Misery loves company and worriers will do their best to drag you down to their level, as the following story illustrates.

> There were two farmers. One was a pessimist, the other was an optimist.
> The optimist would say, "Wonderful sunshine."
> The pessimist would respond, "Yeah, I'm afraid it's going to scorch the crops."
> The optimist would say, "Fine rain."
> The pessimist would respond, "Yeah, I'm afraid we are going to have a flood."
> One day the optimist said to the pessimist, "Have you seen my new bird dog? He's the finest money can buy."
> The pessimist said, "You mean that mutt I saw penned up behind your house? He don't look like much to me."
> The optimist said, "How about going hunting with me tomorrow?" The pessimist agreed. They went. They shot some ducks. The ducks landed on the pond. The optimist ordered his dog to get the ducks. The dog obediently responded. Instead of swimming in the water after the ducks, the dog walked on top of the water, retrieved the ducks, and walked back on top of the water.
> The optimist turned to the pessimist and said, "Now, what do you think of that?"
> Whereupon the pessimist replied, "Hmmm, he can't swim, can he?"

In the strength of God, control your thoughts. Let them be regulated according to the will of God. Such thoughts will lead to inner poise that is a shield against worry.

11

Poise Through Self-Control

Study the records of those whom the world calls great and you will observe that every one of them possesses this quality of self-control.

Many homes are wrecked through lack of self-control. Only God knows the number of churches whose testimonies have been irreparably neutralized simply because of this prevalent lack of self-control among the leadership. Businessmen by the thousands who are capable and qualified in every other respect receive only a fraction of their income potential due to this lack of self-control.

Never retaliate against your enemies. In so doing you may force them to pay the price of grief, but the resultant price of your own grief will be greater. The Bible tells us that we must love our enemies (Matthew 5:44).

While you are hating your enemies you are giving them the sovereignty of your own life. You are literally forcing them to dominate you. For instance, here is a man who has wronged you. You loathe him. Your loathing becomes a festering personality-sore. You so detest him you would not welcome him into your home. You would not permit him to fraternize with your relatives. You would not invite him to eat at your table or spend the night in your guest room. Yet, all the time, while you are hating him you are "entertaining" him in your bloodstream, in your brain cells, in your nerve fibers, in your muscles, and in the marrow of your bones. You are giving him power over your sleep, power over your blood pressure, power over your health, power over your happiness. You are *insisting* that he destroy your body and disintegrate your effectiveness. *Tragic!*

Some years ago *Life* carried an article on high blood pressure. In that article the statement was made that the chief personality trait of people with high blood pressure is resentment. What a price to pay for lack of self-control! They are paying financially in doctors' bills and medical assistance. They are paying emotionally with shattered nerves. They are paying in reduced efficiency resulting in decreased income. They are paying domestically in strife in the home resulting from the projection of their bitterness and misery. *What a price!*

Learn a lesson from our Lord in whose steps we are commanded to follow:

> Who, when he was reviled, reviled not again; when he suffered, he threatened not; but committed himself to him that judgeth righteously (1 Peter 2:23).

Well did the wise Solomon say:

> Better . . . is he that ruleth his spirit than he that taketh a city (Proverbs 16:32b).

Reflect for a moment upon the poise of the immortal Abraham Lincoln. In the anguish of his most grief-producing hours, he exercised poise. Had it not been for this quality it is doubtful that the war between the states would have ended in victory for the Union Army. It is highly doubtful his name would have been immortalized had it not been for this magnificent quality. Men in his own cabinet were disloyal to him, trying on several occasions to discredit him. To his back they made light of him, scoffed at his limited education, and sneered at his rustic ways. Realizing that their disloyalty was to him personally, and realizing further that they possessed qualities making them essential to our nation, the ex-railsplitter exercised self-control, disregarding the objectional characteristics of these colleagues.

In attaining the mastery of self-control you must learn how to *conquer criticism.* I do not mean that you can avoid criticism. Nor do I mean that you can subdue criticism. You can conquer it, however, with respect to its relationship *to you* personally.

Once again follow the example of our Lord who answered His critics so often with silence. Our Lord defended other people. He defended the Word of God. He defended the work of His Heavenly Father. He defended little children. *He never defended Himself!*

Usually you will find it wise not to answer your critics.

> Answer not a fool according to his folly, lest thou also be like unto him (Proverbs 26:4).

Your friends don't need an answer and your enemies won't believe the answer.

Unjust criticism is often a disguised compliment. It often indicates that you have excited the jealousy and envy of the critic. As the old adage goes, "No one ever kicks a dead dog."

It is wise to listen to criticism of yourself, but do it objectively. While listening, don't allow yourself to become emotionally involved. Sometimes you can profit greatly. If the criticism is just, do something about it. If the criticism is unjust, put it where you put your other garbage.

Clergyman are often criticized! If the minister wears a black suit, the critics say, "Who does he think he is—Digger O'Dell?" If he wears a sport coat, the critics question, "What is he trying to do, imitate a movie star?" If he has five children they respond, "He can't afford such a family. Why doesn't he use better sense?" If he has only one child they quip, "Doesn't he know the Bible says that we are to be 'fruitful and multiply'?" If he visits the poor they say he is showing off. If he visits the rich they say he is playing politics. If he drives a Buick they say he ought to drive a car priced within his means. If he drives a Volkswagen, they say, "What's he trying to do, embarrass us by letting people think we don't pay him enough?" If he preaches 30 minutes, they say he is long-winded. If he preaches 20 minutes they say, "What's the matter, didn't he study last week?" If he goes away to conduct meetings in another church they complain, "He ought to stay home and take care of the flock." If he stays home and never goes away, they howl, "What's the matter, doesn't anyone else want him either?" My father gave me some good advice when I entered the ministry. He said, "John, listen to what people say when they are mad. That's what they really mean."

A man flies off the handle. He says some nasty things. After he cools down he comes back and says, "I really didn't mean that." Of course he meant it! If he had not thought it, he would not have said it, for God's Word makes it clear that "Out of the abundance of the heart the mouth speaketh" (Matthew 12:34b). He didn't draw those words and thoughts out of thin air. They were in his heart.

While I am no disciple of Freud, I do belive in the so-called Freudian slips. When a person writes me a letter in longhand and he crosses out one word and writes down another, I may spend 15 or 20 minutes holding that letter up to the light trying to decipher the word crossed out. In all probability that was what he really meant.

When you respond to criticism volcanically, you lose possession of many of your faculties so that your thoughts become inaccurate, your decisions unwise, and your words regrettable.

Let me tell you a little habit I have formed which has served me well. By nature I am very explosive. After all, I am half Syrian and people from that part of the world are not usually phlegmatic. When God called me into the ministry, He impressed upon me the fact that by His grace my spirit must be completely dominated by Him if I were to be an effective ambassador of the Court of Heaven. I memorized and meditated upon 2 Timothy 2:24,25.

> And the servant of the Lord must not strive; but be gentle unto all men, apt to teach, patient. In meekness instructing those that oppose themselves; if God peradventure will give them repentance to the acknowledging of the truth.

Now here is the procedure I have followed when the provocation of unjust criticism has sorely tempted me to lose my head. Through sheer conscious effort I listen objectively. I look at the person who is venting his anger, but I do not see him, for in my mind's eye I am watching a moving picture. A huge elephant is walking down the street. I picture myself as that elephant. Over by the curb (and I am inclined sometimes to think, in the gutter) there's a little ant who is spitting at the elephant. Rather ludicrous, you say. Precisely. It helps my sense of humor. Now then, does the elephant stop and threaten the ant? Of course not. The elephant is unaware of the puny efforts of this pompous ant.

All I can say is that this certainly works for me and I have no copyright on it. It keeps me in complete possession of my faculties so that I can think clearly and quickly, talk judiciously, and act wisely.

An American statesman was once quoted as saying, "Never lose your temper except when you do it on purpose." That's a good statement and one that will bear much thought.

Let's go back to Abraham Lincoln for just a moment. While he was an occupant of the White House, some loquacious "smut-sprayers" and "character assassinators" spread the rumor that he was living with a black woman. What did the President do? Nothing. This man of poise had learned that in a fight with a skunk you might win the fight, but you will smell awful!

If as you've been reading these last few paragraphs you have caught yourself chuckling a time or two, good. Don't take yourself too seriously.

A vital relationship with God through Christ will result in self-control and you will refuse to respond to criticism with smug complacence, worldly courtesy, patronizing condescension, or vindictive retaliation. You will respond with *love* which is not compatible with fear, the basis of worry.

> There is no fear in love; but perfect love casteth
> out fear: because fear hath torment. He that feareth
> is not made perfect in love (1 John 4:18).

12

Poise Through Enthusiasm

Once again let me remind you that by poise we are referring to gentleness, fairness, and congeniality of spirit.

Enthusiasm is an indispensable ingredient. Some pseudointellectuals may take exception to this. I reply simply that most of what we do is done on the basis of emotional impulse rather than intellectual impulse. I do not love my next-door neighbor because of an intellectual theory regarding him. Rather I love him because of an emotional impulse. You did not buy that insurance policy because you intend to die tomorrow and because through intellectual activity you arrived at that sobering possibility. The main inducement was strictly emotional. You saw your family destitute and in want because of inadequate material resources. It was the emotional reaction of this that led you to buy the insurance policy. You go to a football game. There you can tell no difference in behavior between the spectator with a third-grade education and the one with several doctoral degrees. They both respond emotionally, with enthusiasm.

One of my hobbies is reading books on salesmanship. I have a collection of over 40. Without exception each book on salesmanship underscores enthusiasm as an essential quality for success.

The leaders of this world always have been and are men of enthusiasm. Adolph Hitler knew the power of enthusiasm. His formula for speaking was "Say it simply. Say it often. *Make it burn.*" And the Austrian "paper hanger" became a world figure who could not be ignored. Paul the apostle was a man of enthusiasm as his own autobiographical remarks in Galatians 1:14 and Acts 22:3 attest. He was so enthusiastic about the gospel he preached that some of the people in Corinth accused him of madness (2 Corinthians 5:13).

The man who never wonders at anything never does anything wonderful. That partially explains why the work of the Lord suffers so across the land. Thousands of people who profess a relationship with God through Jesus Christ have apparently failed to grasp what Christ has done for us and what are our privileges in Him. Therefore they come to church on Sunday morning with a face long enough to eat ice cream out of a pipe. You could ruin the greatest football team in the nation if you would fill the grandstands for four consecutive games with the average Sunday morning congregation.

No wonder communism spreads while the religion of Jesus Christ fails to keep pace with the population increase of the world. One thing you must say for the Communists—they are enthusiastic about their cause. Next Sunday when you go to church, watch the average person as he comes in. He shuffles along dragging his lower lip behind him. Then he slides into the pew and hangs his lower lip over the pew in front of him. He looks as happy as the skull and crossbones on an iodine bottle. No wonder he has no peace of mind. Remember chapter 5. You cannot act one way and feel another way. When you act sour, you are sour.

Some people who profess "religion" have talked about it for so long in negative terms and in pessimistic platitudes that a distorted concept has made its way into the thinking of the people whom they influence.

I heard of a man who walked into a hotel lobby and stood beside another man at the room clerk's counter. The fellow eyed his neighbor for a moment and then could not restrain himself from asking, "Are you a preacher?"

"No," said the neighbor, "I've just been sick!"

And I can well understand the little girl who came home from Sunday school and going up to Betsy, the mule, lovingly stroked her long head and said, "Bless you, Betsy, you must be a wonderful Christian. You look just like Grandma."

Not only is a lack of enthusiasm ruinous to the work of the Lord, it is also ruinous to happiness in the home, success in business, the making and keeping of friends, and achievement in any field.

There is no such thing as a well-adjusted personality apart from enthusiasm. There is no such thing as a satisfactory social relationship apart from enthusiasm. You reap what you sow. You sow the wind and you get the whirlwind. You sow a deadpan expression and that is exactly what you reap from the people with whom you associate. For what you give you receive in kind, but in greater degree. That is a fact that cannot be denied.

It was my privilege to have an interview with Ray Jenkins, the brilliant lawyer from Knoxville, Tennessee, who presided over the Army-McCarthy hearings. In the course of conversation I asked him his formula for success in speaking. He mentioned several things, but one thing remains paramount in my mind. "Don't ever speak on a subject about which you are not totally enthused." This statement came from the lips of a man who is considered by the people of Tennessee, and of the United States for that matter, to be one of America's outstanding trial lawyers.

> Whatsoever thy hand findeth to do, do it with thy might; for there is no work, nor device, nor knowledge, nor wisdom, in the grave, whither thou goest (Ecclesiastes 9:10).

Enthusiasm is essential to *industry* which is discussed in chapter 18. Enthusiasm is like steam. It impels action. Many people never become enthusiastic over anything, therefore they never *do* anything. Their lives become idle and negative and worrisome.

Enthusiasm tones up the whole life. You know men, and so do I, who constantly complain that they don't get enough sleep. They lament that they wake up every morning feeling as tired as when they went to bed. But what happens when they plan a fishing trip? They are awake before the alarm sounds at four o'clock in the morning—and feeling great! The explanation? Enthusiasm! All things being equal, the person who is enthusiastic turns out three and four times as much work as the person who is listless.

No great work has ever been done without enthusiasm. I give to God all the glory for the ministry of Billy Sunday. But let me state it flatly. Had it not been for his enthusiasm it is highly doubtful he would have so influenced this nation and even the world through a ministry that could not be ignored. Brother, he was enthusiastic!

To be sure, some people seem to be born with a greater capacity for enthusiasm than others. However, this is a quality that can be developed. It is developed by focusing the mind upon a worthwhile goal until the attainment of that goal becomes your "Magnificent Obsession."

The salesmen who succeed are enthusiastic salesmen. Musicians who succeed are enthusiastic musicians. Watch Leonard Bernstein on television! Have you not heard of some musicians who became so engrossed in their practice that they forgot even to take their meals? I submit to you that their achievements would be impossible without enthusiasm.

Enthusiasm leads to achievement. A sense of achievement—an awareness of accomplishment—is indispensable to poise and to peace.

If you go about your daily responsibilities in a listless and lackadaisical spirit devoid of enthusiasm, you are doomed to failure. Your failure will create anxiety and worry. Anxiety and worry will create failure. Thus you become the duped victim of a vicious cycle.

Remember that you cannot focus your attention upon two thoughts at the same time. When you are enthused, you are focusing your attention upon thoughts that crowd out the thoughts producing fears and worry.

See what Paul suffered:

> Of the Jews five times received I forty stripes save one.
>
> Thrice was I beaten with rods, once was I stoned, thrice I suffered shipwreck, a night and a day I have been in the deep;
>
> In journeyings often, in perils of waters, in perils of robbers, in perils by mine own countrymen, in

perils by the heathen, in perils in the city, in perils in the wilderness, in perils in the sea, in perils among false brethren;

In weariness and painfulness, in watchings often, in hunger and thirst, in fastings often, in cold and nakedness.

Beside those things that are without, that which cometh upon me daily, the care of all the churches (2 Corinthians 11:24-28).

Did he worry? Did he fret? No! A godly enthusiasm delivered him from self-pity and worry. Ponder his poise—poise through enthusiasm.

We are troubled on every side, yet not distressed; we are perplexed, but not in despair;

Persecuted, but not forsaken; cast down, but not destroyed;

For which cause we faint not; but though our outward man perish, yet the inward man is renewed day by day.

For our light affliction, which is but for a moment, worketh for us a far more exceeding and eternal weight of glory (2 Corinthians 4:8,9,16,17).

13

Poise Through Relaxation

Poise and relaxation go together like bread and butter and ham and eggs. You cannot maintain poise while you are tense. It is also true that you cannot relax and worry at the same time. Read the books *Progressive Relaxation* and *You Must Relax* by Dr. Edmund Jacobson.

Learn how to work under pressure without working under tension. This is possible if you have periodic breaks in your activities. That is, periodic rest periods. The rest may be a *change* in activity. It is only by this procedure that your heart continues to work for 70 years or so. And believe me, it *works.* It pumps enough blood through your body every 24 hours to fill a railway tanker. Every day it exerts as much effort as it would take to shovel 20 tons of gravel onto a platform as high as your waist.

If you think to excuse your tension on the alleged (and fanciful) basis of your responsibilities, forget it! No one has had the responsibilities that fell upon our blessed Lord. If anyone had cause for tension, He had. Yet He always remained relaxed. Even when they sought to kill Him, He moved quietly and unhurriedly out of their midst. Can you possibly picture our Lord in a frenzied hurry? To be sure, however, there was a definiteness to His walk and to His talk and to the totality of His activities. He said,

> I must work the works of him that sent me, while it is day: The night cometh, when no man can work (John 9:4).

Yet despite that fact, on more than one occasion when pressured by others, He said in substance, "My opportunity is not yet come. The time is not fulfilled." He is our Exemplar

91

in poise through relaxation. Hear Him as He says, "Come ye yourselves apart into a desert place, and rest a while . . ." (Mark 6:31).

Well did Vance Havner say, "The Lord told His disciples, 'Come ye apart and rest awhile,' What He meant was, 'Come ye apart and rest awhile or come ye apart.' " Well spoken words, Dr. Havner! It says that many were coming and going so they didn't have enough leisure to eat decently. You know some people think that they are busy when they are only nervous—rather, when they are only mentally maladjusted.

Now let us repeat J. B. Phillips' translation of verse 6:

> Don't worry over anything whatever; tell God every detail of your needs in earnest and thankful prayer, and the peace of God, which transcends human understanding, will keep constant guard over your hearts and minds as they rest in Christ Jesus (Philippians 4:6).

There is a rhythm, a cadence in all of nature. Plants reproduce themselves in their seasons and men in their generation. There is a rhythm, a cadence in all the action of nature—in our breathing, in the ebbing and flowing of the tide, in the rising and setting of the sun. One of the earmarks of the amateur musician is that he does not give proper observance to the rests.

Thomas Edison got by on four hours' sleep a day, we are told. However, he had the ability to "snooze" at almost any hour of the day or night. He was relaxed at all times. One of the most prominent of our contemporary psychologists has suggested that we need rest for the body and sleep for the mind. He goes on further to say that the man who stays free of psychic tensions gets by on less sleep than the man who gets tied up in knots.

The last year that Dr. Robert G. Lee was President of the Southern Baptist Convention he was in his 60's. During that year he traveled over 150,000 miles, built an auditorium that cost over one and a half million dollars, and received over

1200 new members into the 9000-member Bellevue Baptist Church in Memphis, Tennessee, of which he was pastor.

One of his members, a prominent Memphis surgeon, Dr. J. Murray Davis, told me that the secret of Dr. Lee's output was his capacity to relax. Dr. Davis said, "It is incredible how this man maintains such a pace despite his years." Then the surgeon recounted this incident in the life of Dr. Lee:

> One Sunday morning I went to make my hospital visits at six o'clock. Dr. Lee was also at the hospital visiting. He then taught our Sunday school class that morning and followed that by the delivery of one of his matchless sermons at the 11 o'clock hour. Immediately after the morning service he flew by chartered plane to Longview, Texas, where he delivered a baccalaureate address Sunday afternoon. He flew back to Memphis in time to speak at a special assembly of the Baptist Training Union in our church. Following that he delivered the evening message at the 7:30 evangelistic hour. After the benediction of the evening service he rushed to the airport where he boarded a plane for California. He flew all night and spoke Monday night to a large convocation in California.

What a pace! Remember: This was when Dr. Lee was in his 60's.

For over a quarter of a century Dr. Lee averaged more than ten visits a day. He preached in his own church a minimum of three times a week and he taught a Sunday school class 44 Sundays out of every year. After he was 40 years of age he built a church from a membership of 1300 to a membership of more than 9000 while all the time traveling and preaching outside his own city nearly as often as an evangelist. The secret? He knew how to relax! He knew how to pace himself! He worked under pressure without working under tension. Now in his 80's he probably preaches as often (if not more often) as any of our contemporary preachers.

Learn the rhythm of successful living. When you work, work. When you rest, rest.

When my father was 62 years of age he pastored a vigorous church in New York State. He slept only a few hours a night. He walked two miles a day. He was one of the best paddleball players in Binghamton, New York, and all his opponents were under 35. On his sixtieth birthday he played two sets of tennis. How did he do it? He knew how to relax.

On several occasions, when visiting him, I had some amusing experiences. He sat in his high-back rocking chair, and I sat across from him. Right in the middle of our conversation he said, "You must excuse me, son. I am going to take a few minutes' snooze." He laid his head back and slept (I have timed him, and he has slept for seven minutes!). Opening his eyes and returning to his alert form, he said, "All right, now. Where were we?"

Most great achievers maintain the practice of having a nap sometime during the day. It has been proved that a person will fare better with six hours of sleep at night and an hour of sleep every afternoon than with eight hours of sleep at night with no break in the day.

As a young man I realized that if I were to be productive, I would have to master the ability to relax and to sleep. I worked at it assiduously. In the late 1960's, I boarded Northwest flight 7 from Seattle to Tokyo. The now retired head of World Vision, Dr. Ted Engstrom, was on the same flight. He said, "John, people tell me that you can sleep like a baby on these flights, and you don't even take a sleeping pill. I don't believe it."

I grinned and said, "Well, Ted, I'm grateful to God. It's true."

Our flight lifted off. We had a meal, after which I read a paper and thumbed through a magazine. About an hour and a half out of Seattle, I stretched across the three seats and laid my head on three pillows just under the window. I slept like a baby until 30 minutes out of Tokyo. Ted couldn't believe it. I had not taken any sleeping pill.

In the late 1970's, my young colleague, Dr. Michael Youssef, and I were waiting for the delayed takeoff of a Pan American flight from Miami to Rio de Janeiro. Our destination was Sao Paulo, where I was to lead a seminar the following day. Finally, at 11 o'clock at night, the plane started rumbling down the runway. I turned to Michael and said, "I'm going to turn on this penlight and do some reading." In what seemed to be just a matter of moments, I was aware that the plane was still rumbling down the runway. I turned to Michael and said, "When in the world are we going to take off?" It was only the grace of God that kept him from reverting to his preconversion vocabulary. He was frustrated! He said, "This is Caracas, Venezuela. You have been sleeping so hard since we left Miami that we couldn't even shake you awake for the meal."

We stayed on the ground in Caracas for an hour. I then slept the four hours from Caracas to Rio de Janeiro. We made a quick transfer flight to Sao Paulo. I cleaned up, shaved, combed my hair. When we disembarked in Sao Paulo, I was ready for a full day's work.

Michael said, "Chief, I am willing to go anywhere with you, but the next time, I'm going to leave two days early."

I said to him what I've said to people all over the world, "One of the best investments of discipline and effort you can make is in learning how to relax so that you can get proper rest, whether it be in a full eight hours end to end, or whether it be six hours with snoozes throughout the day, or whatever is the best for you."

There's no way that I could have maintained my schedule over the past 22 years had I not learned the secret of relaxation. In 22 years I have made 63 trips around the world; written eight books and hundreds of inches of copy for brochures, appeal letters, and magazine articles; averaged a speech situation nearly once a day; administrated an organization that has offices in all parts of the world; and maintained my own personal study habits and responsibilities. Were it not for my ability to relax, I would be a physical and emotional basket case by this time. At an age that some consider appropriate for retirement, I thank God I'm still able to function with a great deal of energy and zest, but relaxation is one of the keys.

Relaxation is a component of poise.

The soil of tension and frenzy is productive of the plant of worry. Therefore, ask God to help you to develop poise through relaxation.

14

Poise Through Scheduling

By scheduling your activities you will make great strides toward victory in the matter of relaxation.

Scheduling leads to relaxation because it defeats frenzy and hurry. Scheduling and regularity go together. These infer order and system which are the best antidotes to hurry. Hurry is symptomatic of a weak mind, or at least a weakly organized mind. Without scheduling and organization there is foolish haste which leads to glaring mistakes which in turn lead to discouragement and tension.

Let me suggest that you once again read the autobiography of Benjamin Franklin in which he tells of his effort to master the 13 virtues. He was past 80 years of age when he wrote the autobiography and after passing the four-score year mark he confided that order was the one virtue he had never been able to conquer. It is probably one of the most difficult habits to perfect.

Yet order is so important. Through disorganization we do not know where we are and there is always fear of the unknown. Worry, like a buzzard, preys upon the carrion of the disorganized mind.

I was told of a state hospital in Illinois. One day one of the inmates ran out of the gate and down the road as fast as he could run. The orderly chased him, caught him, and brought him back. The next day another inmate did exactly the same thing with the same result. That happened ten successive days with ten different inmates. Now, if the ten inmates had fled at the same time, and if each had run in a different direction, nine of them would have escaped. However, they were not *organized*. That's why they were in the institution!

Plan your work and work your plan. Ask God for the wisdom to help you plan your work and then ask God for the grace to enable you to work your plan. "The Lord is near." Call upon Him for the needed wisdom and grace.

Just as He led Nehemiah to plan for and to organize the work of the building of the wall around Jerusalem and just as He enabled Nehemiah and the brethren to work the plan—despite unspeakable opposition—so the Lord will enable you, if you will but call upon Him, to so plan your work and work your plan that you will fulfill the divine injunction to be "always abounding in the work of the Lord."

Fatigue is caused mostly by boredom. When you have no order—when you have failed to schedule your activities—you lack the awareness of accomplishment. Conversely, when you have wisely scheduled your activities under the leadership of the Holy Spirit, and when in His strength you are performing your responsibilities on schedule, you get the lift that comes from the awareness of accomplishment. There is nothing more invigorating than the knowledge of tasks efficiently completed, and there is nothing more dispiriting than the knowledge of unfulfilled responsibilities.

Paul enjoins us to be "redeeming the time, for the days are evil." By His grace and in His strength we will fulfill our responsibility to redeem the time and at the same time we will conquer worry through poise by scheduling.

Korean Presbyterians invited me to be the evangelist in 1970 for the Seventh Decade Spiritual Revolution Crusade. The chairman was Dr. Kyung Chik Han, pastor of the world's largest Presbyterian Church . . . the Young Nak (meaning "eternal joy") Church in Seoul. The crusade was of three weeks' duration, with one week in each of three cities—Pusan, Taegu, and Seoul.

For 21 days I was honored to be in the company of this world leader.

Twice dispossessed of all—literally *all*—his earthly goods, he had known the scourge of Japan's cruel occupation in the 40's and North Korea's atheistic terrorism in the 50's.

In 1956, with 27 North Korean refugees, Dr. Han founded the Young Nak Church. Just after the outer structure of the new sanctuary was completed, the North Koreans stormed across the 38th parallel and into Seoul, driving freedomloving Koreans southward . . . and ultimately nearly into the sea. The new sanctuary was used by the North Koreans as an ammunition depot.

Dr. Han and his people established three other Young Nak churches during their southern exile.

Back in Seoul in 1953, the work continued, and the statistics are impressive. The membership climbed to more than 16,000 by 1972. More than 100 daughter churches were established. Schools, orphanages, senior citizens' quarters, summer camp and spiritual retreat grounds and facilities, special ministries among the military groups, are but a few of the projects launched under Dr. Han's leadership.

Yet, the dear man never appears harried or hurried. I watched for three weeks—in vain, I might add—for any sign of pique or impatience.

Dr. Han met with his people every morning for the five o'clock to six o'clock dawn prayer meeting. What a way to start every day!

His life was and is a model of quiet achievement . . . for Christ. He is the master teacher of "The Stewardship of Time." I have heard him. Better, I have watched him!

He so schedules himself, so plans his work and works his plan, that without frenzy he discharges herculean responsibilities.

He knows God has given him adequate time to achieve all that lies within the divine will. In complete dependence upon the Holy Spirit of God, he moves peacefully and productively.

Relaxed and gracious, he infuses a "God is in His heaven, so fear not" mood into the room.

Dr. Han's life is a symphony of poise. The atmosphere of his home is the vestibule to heaven. Fellowship with this man of God bestows its own special benediction.

The Lord gives us the ability and the time to do *everything* He expects us to do. We have an obligation and privilege to utilize these God-given resources to the end that His will for us be fulfilled. Fulfillment of His will for us honors God and tends to dispel worry.

God help us to be able to say as our Lord while yet on earth could say:

> I have finished the work which thou gavest me to do (John 17:4b).

15

Poise Through Sidelines

Probably a preferable word to sidelines would be diversions. Beauty consists of contrasts, shades, varieties, and changes. "Variety is the spice of life."

The apostle Paul was not only a preacher; he was also a logician. Apparently he was interested in athletics, because he alluded to athletics many times in his epistles. Furthermore, his reference to Greek poets in Acts 17 seems to indicate he was conversant with poetry. Certainly no one could deny that he was also a master at understanding human nature.

David the king was a sportsman, a poet, a musician, a militarist, and a philosopher. And who could adequately evaluate the multiplicity of interests maintained by his son Solomon?

> And he spake three thousand proverbs: and his songs were a thousand and five.
> And he spake of trees, from the cedar tree that is in Lebanon even unto the hyssop that springeth out of the wall: he spake also of beasts, and of fowl, and of creeping things, and of fishes (1 Kings 4:32,33).

You will see here that Solomon was a sage—"he spake three thousand proverbs." He was a musician and poet—"and his songs were a thousand and five." He was a horticulturist—"and he spake of trees from the cedar tree that is in Lebanon even unto the hyssop that springeth out of the wall." He was an expert in animal husbandry—"he spake also of beasts." He was an ornithologist—"he spake of fowl." He was an entomologist—he spake "of creeping things." He was a piscatologist—he spake "of fishes."

Take the example of our own Lord. Study His parables and you will conclude that He was interested in and conversant with all phenomena and activities. Jesus was the Master Psychologist. He understood the laws of agriculture and horticulture. Our Lord displayed great interest in the sea and in fishing. He certainly understood the laws of anatomy and body function. He was an ornithologist and He knew animal husbandry.

Because of the broad interests of our Lord, men of every strata of society and rank of individuality and echelon of culture listened to Him with absorption. He could appeal to the religious and cultured and educated Nicodemus equally as well as He could appeal to the woman of ill repute from Samaria.

Diversion of interests, a hobby, or an avocation effectuate the balance that leads to poise. They bring the other dimensions into life that give life real perspective.

When Paul the apostle was forced out of Berea because of persecution and a threat to his life, he did not go to Athens and brood. He kept busy. In Athens he went down to the marketplace and listened to the dialogues of the philosophers. He studied the habit patterns of the Athenians. There he discovered their basic interests and their mental behavior. This turned out to be fruitful in the extreme. It wasn't long until they insisted that he go to Areopagus—to the top of Mars Hill—where only the great orators and the celebrities were permitted to speak. There he delivered the most masterful sermon ever preached by any man (our Lord excepted, of course). Through diversion he refused to give himself time to brood over his lot as a persecuted and a hounded preacher of the Word.

No man can honor God in a maximum way whose only interests are within the boundaries of a narrow and specialized field. Without a variety of interests you will not maintain any interest for long.

You see, this works hand in glove with the already mentioned importance of becoming genuinely interested in other people.

The brilliant pulpit orator from Louisiana, Dr. James W. Middleton, has been through enough to drive to despair and shatter the nerves of five rugged men. Recently he was out of his pulpit for nearly a year because of throat difficulties that subjected him to the surgeon's scalpel on two different occasions. His entire ministry seemed to be in jeopardy. Yet, as you listen to that matchless preacher, you are at once impressed with his poise—his sense of inner peace. As you hear that magnificiently controlled bass voice rising and falling, whispering and roaring, declaiming and appealing, like a mighty four-manual pipe organ under the domination of a master, you detect complete mastery. I am convinced that one of the explanations of his self-control and poise lies in his hobbies, one of which is horticulture. He has performed some amazing grafts of plants in tree stumps. He, too, is a sportsman—a fisherman and a hunter of no mean ability.

Dr. Roy O. McClain, former pastor of the First Baptist Church of Atlanta, Georgia, and selected some years ago by *Time* as one of the ten outstanding American clergymen, had several hobbies, among which were the raising of Shetland ponies, painting, the playing of the organ, and woodworking. These hobbies served as a balance wheel enabling him to honor the Lord in a maximum way through unruffled poise even though he was saddled with the titantic task of pastoring the largest congregation in the state of Georgia.

I seriously doubt Australian Dr. Ernest Watson the dean of Haggai Institute could maintain his Spirit-set pace were it not for the diversion he finds in swimming, music, and other outside interests.

President Eisenhower found diversion in painting and in golf.

The late Dr. Harry A. Ironside, who was deprived of an education past the eighth grade (I should say he was deprived of "schooling" past the eighth grade. His education was equivalent to that required to earn several doctor's degrees) found his diversion in poetry and in learning Greek and Chinese.

Dr. J. C. Massee, now deceased, formerly one of the nation's outstanding ministers, evangelists, and seminary professors, maintained a youthfulness and a virility usually associated with a man half his years. He found diversion in the study of words and in gardening, to mention but two of his many interests. When I last talked with him, I was uplifted and challenged by his spirit. When many men at his age (the mid-80's) would be complaining and dawdling, he was productively active. In discussing the blessings of the Lord upon his life, he said to me in a triumphant note, "My lines have fallen in pleasant places" (cf. Psalm 16:6).

You will notice that I have mentioned a number of clergymen. The reason for this is that ministers, more than any other group of men, have reason to get bogged down in the mire of routine responsibilities. They are on call 24 hours a day, seven days a week. They never have the satisfaction of knowing that everything is done. There is always another person to visit, another letter to write, another message to prepare. No wonder Dr. Wesley Schrader wrote the article appearing in *Life* some years ago on "Why Ministers Are Cracking Up."

For years I had looked with envy on people who did downhill skiing. I felt I could not afford the cost, and I knew, without a shadow of a doubt, I could not afford the time. However, I set my goal to take up skiing at 63. On my sixty-third birthday I drove to Hopfgarten, Austria, and for the next two-and-a-half weeks, I enjoyed the professional excellence of Austria's proverbial ski geniuses. In seven days, I was coming down the steepest slope of Hopfgarten Mountain. In nine days, I was feeling much more comfortable. Before I left, my Austrian friends gave me a videotape made by Austria's Department of Ski Instruction so that during the summer months I could rehearse the various moves by watching the video.

This is the first time I have had an athletic sideline to which I have devoted energy, enthusiasm, and resources. I tell you frankly that this sideline, skiing, has done as much to undergird inner poise and serenity as anything I have ever done.

For one thing, you cannot come down a steep ski slope and think about anything else except skiing. It's a marvelous way to force yourself to brush aside the multitude of energy-sapping little problems that are a part of daily living.

I'm not suggesting that you take up the sideline of skiing. I am suggesting that you find some sideline to which you can give wholehearted enthusiasm—a sideline that helps you to relax and that reinforces inner poise. Some women find diversion in mastering the art of cooking, in interior decorating, in gardening, in music, in writing, in all types of sports, and in a host of other interests.

Let me suggest that for added stimulus along this line you read Marie Beynon Ray's book *How Never to Get Tired.*

In Mark 6:31 when Jesus said to the apostles, "Come ye apart and rest awhile," the context shows that they did not go apart for a time of inactivity. Rather they went out to eat and then they engaged in a different form of activity. More times than not, rest is effectuated not by cessation of activity, but by change in the activity.

Jesus was always busy about His Father's business even though the pattern of His activity changed often.

Some men, it is true, find within the framework of their calling enough variation so that they maintain the poise that comes through diversion within the confines of their calling. This was true of Dr. George W. Truett.

The world-famed industrialist, the late R. G. LeTourneau, had an important appointment in his plant at Toccoa, Georgia. While in flight to Georgia the landing gear of his plane stuck. The pilot radioed ahead to the Anderson, South Carolina, airport and told them of his plight. Ambulances and a rescue squad rushed to the airport. The newsmen and the cameramen were on the spot ready to cover the landing. They made a good crash landing. When Mr. LeTourneau got out of the plane his first words, in substance, were, "Where's the car? Where's the car? I am already late for my appointment in Toccoa. Can you get me a car immediately?"

There is poise. I asked him one time when he took his

vacation. He said, "I never take a vacation. My work is my play and you never need a vacation from play." There was a man who through Christ and wise self-discipline learned the poise that conquers worry.

16

Poise Through Seizing the Day

In other words, live for today!

The songwriter D. W. Whittle understood this truth when he wrote,

Moment by moment I'm kept in His love,
Moment by moment I've help from above.
Looking to Jesus, till glory doth shine;
Moment by moment, Oh, Lord, I am thine.

The trouble with many people is that instead of "looking to Jesus" they are looking to tomorrow.

Yesterday is a cashed check and cannot be negotiated. Tomorrow is a promissory note and cannot be utilized today. Today is cash in hand. Spend it wisely.

> This is the day which the Lord hath made; we will rejoice and be glad in it (Psalm 118:24).

Lowell Thomas had these words framed and hung on the walls of his broadcasting studio at his farm so that he could see them often.

If this verse is the convicton of your heart, it is impossible for you to worry.

Don't live in the past. On the other hand, don't live in the future. Paul was in the habit of "forgetting those things which are behind" (Philippians 3:13). While it is true that he was striving for future mastery, Philippians 3:12-14 makes it clear that his emphasis was on his opportunities and responsibilities during the present.

Give every moment your all. Give your entire attention to the work at hand, the person with whom you are talking or dealing. The Lord grants us time only in the quantity that we can use it—one moment at a time.

There is an illustration of our responsibility to live one day at a time in the story of the manna in Exodus 16. Now read this passage with special attention to the words that I have italicized.

> This is the thing which the Lord hath commanded, Gather of it every man *according to his eating, an omer for every man, according to the number of your persons* . . .
>
> And the children of Israel did so, and gathered, some more, some less.
>
> And when they did mete it with an omer, he that gathered much had nothing over, and he that gathered little had no lack; they gathered every man according to his eating.
>
> And Moses said, Let no man leave of it till the morning.
>
> Notwithstanding they hearkened not unto Moses; *but some of them left of it until the morning, and it bred worms, and stank* . . . (Exodus 16:16-20).

The Israelites were in need of food. The Lord provided for them a *daily* supply. He did not make available to them a week's supply. If they gathered more than a day's supply, all in excess of their daily requirements rotted. The truth is simply this: In the resources of God made available to you, *live for today.*

Here again our Lord is *the* example. He came to die. Through His death He would set up a kingdom—a kingdom not of this world, but a spiritual kingdom. Said Jesus, "To this end was I born, and for this cause came I into the world" (John 18:37).

The shadow of persecution and death constantly lay across His path. Nevertheless, He lived one day at a time and did not permit the grief, torture, and pain that faced Him to rob Him of perfect composure for today. Little children reveled in His company. Men who conversed with Him were aware of His total absorption with their own problems at that given time. Over and over again we can hear our Lord saying, "My hour is not yet come." In other words, He lived "moment by moment," one day at a time. Observe His matchless poise!

Don't be forever living in the future. As a Christian, look unceasingly for the Blessed Hope and Glorious Appearing of Jesus Christ, but while so doing, don't neglect your present work. Live in such a way that you would never be ashamed to meet Jesus no matter when He would appear.

In Acts 1:6 the followers of our Lord asked:

> Lord, wilt thou at this time restore again the kingdom to Israel?

Consider the answer of our Lord,

> . . . It is not for you to know the times or the seasons, which the Father hath put in his own power. But ye shall receive power, after that the Holy Ghost is come upon you . . . (Acts 1:7,8).

Our Lord replied by showing them that the finest possible preparation they could make for the future was a Spirit-led execution of the present. The proof that the child of God is looking forward to the Second Coming of Christ is made clear by his faithfulness in living *today* for the glory of God.

Montaigne said, "My life has been full of terrible misfortunes, most of which never happened." Many of us might say the same thing. How foolish of us to scuttle our opportunities and waste the privileges of this day which is slipping away with fantastic speed.

John Ruskin had on his desk a simple piece of stone on which was sculptured one word: *today.*

Osler gives good advice when he says, "Banish the future; live only for the hour and its allotted work. . . . Set earnestly at the little task at your elbow . . . our plain duty is "not to see what lies dimly at a distance, but to do what lies clearly at hand.' "

Yes, seize *today!* Richard Baxter left to us sage advice when he said, "Spend your time in nothing which you know must be repented of; in nothing on which you might not claim the blessings of God; in nothing which you could not review with a quiet conscience on your dying bed; in nothing which you might not be safely and properly doing if guests surprise you in the act."

Most of your misery is left over from yesterday or borrowed from tomorrow. In the dynamic of the Holy Spirit determine to live today to the glory of God. This is the day that the Lord has made. Paul would remind you to redeem the time for the days are evil (Ephesians 5:16). God has given you today. He has taken back all your yesterdays. All your tomorrows are still in His keeping.

The Lord graciously blessed us with a precious son. He was paralyzed and able to sit in his wheelchair only with the assistance of full-length body braces. One of the nation's most respected gynecologists and obstetricians brought him into the world. Tragically, this man—overcome by grief—sought to find the answer in a bourbon bottle rather than in the blessed Bible. Due to the doctor's intoxication at the time of delivery, he inexcusably bungled his responsibility. Several of the baby's bones were broken. His leg was pulled out at the growing center. Needless abuse—resulting in hemorrhaging of the brain—was inflicted upon the little fellow. (Let me pause long enough to say that this is no indictment upon doctors. I thank God for doctors. This man was a tragic exception. He was banned from practice in some hospitals, and, as mentioned previously, he committed suicide.)

During the first year of the little lad's life, eight doctors said he could not possibly survive. For the first two years of his life my wife had to feed him every three hours with a Brecht feeder. It took a half hour to prepare for the feeding and it took another half hour to clean up and put him back to bed. Not once during that time did she get out of the house for any diversion whatsoever. Never did she get more than two hours sleep at one time.

My wife, formerly Christine Barker of Bristol, Virginia, had once been acclaimed by some of the nation's leading musicians as one of the outstanding contemporary female vocalists in America. From the time she was 13 she had been popular as a singer—and constantly in the public eye. Hers was the experience of receiving and rejecting some fancy offers with even fancier incomes to marry an aspiring Baptist pastor with no church to pastor!

Then, after five years of marriage, tragedy struck! The whole episode was so unnecessary. From a life of public service she was now marooned within the walls of our home. Her beautiful voice no longer enraptured public audiences with the story of Jesus, but was now silenced, or at best, muted to the subdued humming of lullabies.

Had it not been for her spiritual maturity whereby she laid hold of the resources of God and lived one day at a time, this heart-rending experience would long since have caused an emotional breakdown.

John Edmund, Jr., our little son, lived 24 years and died in 1975. We rejoice that he committed his heart and life to Jesus Christ and gave evidence of a genuine concern for the things of the Lord. I attribute his commitment to Jesus Christ and his wonderful disposition to the sparkling radiance of an emotionally mature, Christ-centered mother who has mastered the discipline of living one day at a time. Never have I—nor has anyone else—heard a word of complaint from her. The people who know her concur that at 35 years of age and after having been subjected to more grief than many people twice her age, she possessed sparkle that would be the envy of any high school senior and the radiance and charm for which any debutante would gladly give a fortune.

Seize today. Live for today. Wring it dry of every opportunity. You have troubles? So do others. So did Paul who said, "Most gladly therefore will I rather glory in my infirmities that the power of Christ may rest upon me" (2 Corinthians 12:9b).

You seize the day. Don't let others seize it for you. Peer pressure in the United States robs too many of their individuality. There's no reason for you to engage in socializing just because that's the excessive pastime of your neighbors. If you want to socialize, if it contributes to your social desires without imposing upon you pressures that are counterproductive, go to it. However, I am appalled at the excessive and superficial socializing in which otherwise free people allow nonproductive activities to enslave them. They permit their minds to be divided between the idea "Is this what I ought to do?" and "What will they think of me if I don't go?" Take control of your own life. Go or don't go.

Because so many allow themselves to become enslaved to this superficial socializing, they never read a book, never memorize a poem, and never take that course at the university night school they had promised themselves they were going to take. In short, they rob themselves of the really important contributions to their lives and influence.

Unfortunately, our society has developed two extreme types of parents: those who abuse their children for whatever reason; and those who become hostage to their children for whatever reason.

In either case, I can assure you that the major reason is the divided mind. And in either case, the children suffer.

Let's take the case of the parents who become hostage to their children. They don't want their children to walk from the front door to the pantry. They must drive them there! Jogging for fitness is in. But for children, walking is out. These parents are determined that whatever the cost, they are to be a spectator at every activity in which the child has a part.

Consequently, we have had a 50-percent increase in obesity among children in the past ten years in the United States. The medical profession says that it's because of too much television and too little exercise.

How many children do you know today who are required to do chores? Even to make up their own beds, help wash the dishes or the car, take care of the lawn, or assist with the housecleaning? I submit to you that in many cases, the parents have split their minds between what they know they ought to do and what their peers are doing down the street.

I was in a vigorous and enjoyable debate with a man from Yorkshire, England. He said, "When I visit your country, I am appalled that so many can't make up their minds."

"What are you talking about?" I protested.

"I'll give you a perfect illustration: Junior asks his mother if he can go to a certain function. His mother then gets on the phone and calls the mothers of all of Junior's neighbors to find out what they are going to do. After having taken a poll of the neighbors, his parents then give Junior the verdict. What a terrible way to rear a lad. They are creating an atmosphere of indecision which is bound to have a deleterious effect on the boy."

I protested vigorously, but in my mind, I knew that more often than I cared to admit, what he said was true. And why do people act in this manner? The divided mind. It's divided between their responsibility as parents and their fear of acting in a way that is not consonant with the responses of the other parents down the street.

In short, they don't seize the day. They let the day—and their peers—seize them. And that does not make for mental health and emotional stability and a serene home life.

You develop greater poise when you determine to take time by the forelock and, under the leadership of God, shake it into obedience and make it your servant instead of your master.

People who worry about their health become hostage to the day instead of seizing the day. A friend told me of his mother who worried for 40 years that she would die of cancer. She died at 73—*from pneumonia!* Tragic! She wasted 40 years worrying about *the wrong thing.* Forty years she brought depression instead of delight to the hearts of her closest friends and members of her family. Forty years she divided her mind and her time between useful pursuits and worrying about cancer. Forty years her testimony for Christ was dimmed and her witness for Christ was diminished in power simply because she refused to live one day at a time—and to live that day to the fullest and to the glory of God.

Read it again:

> This is the day which the Lord hath made; we will rejoice and be glad in it (Psalm 118:24).

17

Poise Through Skill

If you would develop the poise that conquers worry, do everything you do the best you can and learn to master some skill.

The late Dr. M. E. Dodd well said, "Many are twisting a tune out of a hand organ when they ought to be playing a four-manual pipe organ. Many are satisfied to play with mud pies when they ought to be making angel food cakes. Many are crawling when they ought to be running. Many are building shacks when they ought to be building palaces."

First Corinthians 10:31 says:

> Whether therefore ye eat, or drink, or whatso-
> ever ye do, do all to the glory of God.

Therefore if we are going to glorify God, we must do our best. There is no room for mediocrity in the life of the child of God. God deserves and demands our best.

> Hear ye the Master's call, "Give Me thy best!"
> For, be it great or small, That is His test.
> Do then the best you can, Not for reward,
> Not for the praise of men, But for the Lord.
>
> Wait not for men to laud, Heed not their slight;
> Winning the smile of God Brings its delight!
> Aiding the good and true Ne'er goes unblest,
> All that we think or do, Be it the best.
>
> Night soon comes on a pace, Day hastens by:
> Workman and work must face Testing on high.
> Oh, may we in that day Find rest, sweet rest,
> Which God has promised those Who do their best.

Every work for Jesus will be blest,
But He asks from everyone His best,
Our talents may be few, These may be small,
But unto Him is due Our best, our all.

Skill is essential to poise. The speaker who has subjected himself to rigorous discipline until he has perfected the craft of speaking is poised when he speaks. The speaker who has not paid the price of discipline and who comes to the pulpit or to the lectern half-prepared lacks poise. If he has any discernment he is tortured at the conclusion of his message as he reflects upon the mess he made of it. The anxiety produced thereby is totally unnecessary and could have been eliminated if he had simply paid the price in developing the needed skill. The same is true of the doctor, the lawyer, the salesman, the artisan, the athlete, the artist, the cook.

For a professing Christian to do less than his best is inexcusable. The Christian has the motive and has the resources for mastery available.

Tragic it is that there are few great musicians today. Few great orators. Few great financiers. Few great inventors. Thank God, however, there are still some who are willing to soar to the heights of the eagle though they know they will fly alone. For the glory of God and for their own peace of mind they are willing to climb the ladder of achievement even though they know that thorns on the rungs will pierce their feet.

Some time ago I had an interview with one of the greatest speech professors in America. He showed me seven pages of elementary voice exercises which to my amazement, he said he has practiced daily for 40 years. This man cannot tolerate mediocrity.

Paderewski practiced simple finger exercises for hours every day over a period of years. No wonder the musical world was hypnotized into the realm of ecstasy by the charm of his musical mastery.

Edison experimented multiplied hundreds of times before he successfully developed the electric light filament. While he was working on it a scientist in England said that anyone was a fraud who would say the electric light filament was a possibility. But Thomas Edison, who loathed mediocrity, kept on giving his best until success crowned his efforts.

Matthew Henry worked hours every day for 40 years in producing his *Commentaries*. They probably appear on the bookshelves of more clergymen than any other commentary. Why? Because, under God, Matthew Henry gave his best.

Jesus told the parable of the man who started the house but never lived in it. Our Master scorned a task half-done.

William Jennings Bryan for years unrelentingly, tediously, laboriously practiced the art of oratory. He never won a speech contest. Nevertheless he kept on. As a comparative unknown he attended the Democratic National Convention held at the Coliseum in Chicago in 1896. Here the years of self-denial and self-discipline paid off. It was past midnight. The people were weary. Many of them were leaving. He stepped up to the stand and delivered his famous *Cross of Gold* oration. This oration so masterfully delivered by the man who never won a speech contest catapulted him into the position of standard-bearer for the Democratic party. In less than 24 hours he had become a national figure. This mighty man of God had mastered the mechanics of the work for which God had called him and the record of his life is a glittering trophy and an imposing monument to the glory of God.

Peace of mind is dependent upon the awareness of divine approval. When we fail to give God our best, we fail to bring maximum honor and glory to His name. The consciousness of this failure produces anxiety and inner conflict.

There is no poise like the poise that accompanies the knowledge of mastery to the glory of God—mastery effectuated in the power of God.

Whatever may be your personal appraisal of television, I think you must confess with me that it presents one of the most stinging rebukes to the apathy of church leadership. Performers will work day and night to attain mastery in the field of show business. Some time ago, when Kate Smith was on TV, I read that for every hour that she was on TV she spent 18 hours in preparation. At that time she was on five hours a week. For five hours of TV entertainment she willingly worked 90 hours to bring to her viewers the finest programs of which she was capable. She did not have to do this for monentary reasons, for she is reputedly a millionaire several times over.

On the other hand, consider how shoddily we treat the Lord, and by "we" I am referring to professing Christians. Take an example. A soloist gets up to sing. Possibly he has rehearsed that particular number, but more probably he hasn't. He sticks his nose in the crease of the book and has to read every word. Imagine an opera star bound down to script and music! What conclusion do you come to? Yes, that's right. The opera star apparently is more devoted to the mastery of his profession than the average gospel soloist is to the glory of God.

In Philippians 4:13 Paul assures us:

> I can do all things through Christ which strengtheneth me.

You have the resources necessary to do what God requires of you. And in the fulfillment of His requirement you will have poise that conquers anxiety.

We like to do what we know how to do well. You are less likely to worry while you are doing what you like to do. Worry results from a divided mind. When you are doing what you like to do, your mind is occupied with one thing. "This one thing I do," said Paul. Dwight L. Moody said most people would have to alter that and confess, "These 50 things I dabble in."

The high school boy enjoys that sport most which he plays best. The housewife is contentedly happy when in the process of making a cake for which she is famous in the community. Watch Leonard Bernstein on television. For one solid hour he holds a capacity studio audience of hundreds of children spellbound and charms millions of television viewers. He is totally absorbed. Obviously he enjoys it. Why? Because he is probably the world's greatest music teacher when it comes to explaining music to the masses. He apparently likes to do this because he has mastered the skill of doing it well. At the conclusion of the hour, even the television viewers detect that he is nearly exhausted, but supremely happy. Yes, I might add, he is poised.

Our high school principal, who also taught us American history, admonished us over and over again to "learn to do at least one thing better than anyone else can do it."

Have you not had this experience many times? Perhaps it was at a party, or maybe a picnic. You saw someone who seemed absolutely bored—thoroughly disgusted. That individual moped around on the sidelines, refusing to participate in the activities. Then, a game or a sport was proposed, the mention of which brought light into his eyes. He threw himself into that game, into that sport, with everything he had. He was skillful in that activity. Now his body was vibrant. His countenance scintillated. His conversation was spirited. Why? Simply because he was now poised. He was skilled in the particular activity and became congenially involved in the group. His mind was no longer divided. His interests were no longer diffused. Obviously he was supremely happy. The explanation simply lies in the fact that we enjoy doing what we know how to do well.

When Bedan Mbugua of Kenya came to Singapore for the course in advanced leadership, he was a pharmaceutical salesman. During the time in Singapore, he became enamored with the possibility of publishing a magazine that would communicate the gospel of Jesus Christ to people who might never come to church or be interested in religious things.

When he returned to Kenya, he pursued his goal. In less than three years, the magazine he was producing outsold *Time* and *Newsweek* in five of Africa's nations, including Nigeria. He later transferred the ownership and production of the magazine to another party, and he started yet another publication.

His story has been one of ever-increasing successes. He loves the work. He loves it, for one reason, because he's good at it, and he's good at it because he loves it!

I repeat, we like to do what we know how to do well. Bedan Mbugua understands magazine publishing. He understands not only the writing needs, the editorial needs, the demographics of the areas where he intends to sell the magazine, but he also understands the business aspects, marketing techniques, and all of the various elements essential to the production of an influential magazine.

If you would conquer worry, discipline yourself to the point of mastery in the field to which God has called you. It is also well for you to become competent in some other fields. This will redound to God's glory, your happiness, and other people's profit.

Jeremiah says:

> Cursed be he that doeth the work of the Lord deceitfully, (the margin renders it "negligently") and cursed be he that keepeth back his sword from blood (Jeremiah 48:10).

For your own peace of mind, excel in at least one thing. Concentrate all your forces upon some work. Gather in your resources, rally all your faculties, marshal all your energies, focus all your capacities upon mastery in at least one field of endeavor. This is a surefire antidote to the divided mind. Stop scattering your fire. Cease any half-hearted attempts to be superb in everything. Ascertain the will of God for your life. Enlist His help and strength through whom you can do all things. Strive for mastery, and experience worry-killing poise through skill.

18

Poise Through Industry

When you are idle you are subject to destructive thoughts, dangerous impulses, and perilous pressures from without. All these things contribute to anxiety.

Jesus Himself said, "I must work" (John 9:4). Jesus also said, "My Father worketh hitherto and I work" (John 5:17).

Work is divine in its inception. The old adage, "Idleness is the devil's workshop," is true.

Reflect upon the grief that idleness brought David the king. When he should have been in battle, he was home taking it easy. While idling about his palace he saw a sight which stirred his sexual passions. Still idle, he reflected and meditated upon that experience until it festered into the open sin of covetousness and then adultery. Those sins in turn led to the murder of Uriah, the husband of Bathsheba. Before long the entire affair was public knowledge. Talk about anxiety! I have no doubt that David at one point would gladly have died rather than lived through the grief and anxiety produced by the harvest of his idleness.

Paul the apostle had been pursued by hostility at Berea, and it was necessary for him to flee to Athens—alone! In Athens he could have holed up in some private room and felt sorry for himself. He could have brooded over the mistreatment he had suffered for the work of the Lord. He could have said, "I have been laboring night and day in Thessalonica and preaching faithfully in Berea. Now I will take it easy." Not Paul. Immediately he began an investigation of conditions in Athens. After acquainting himself with the conditions in this intellectual metropolis, he began to preach in the synagogue with the Jews and with devout persons in the marketplace daily. Soon his ministry attracted the interest of the philosophers, of the Epicureans, and of the Stoics. They requested a speech from him in which he would set forth his philosophy. He could have responded, "Oh, no. I was stoned and left for dead at Lystra. I was beaten and jailed in Philippi. I have just now been abused in Berea for this very thing—preaching the gospel of the Son of God, whom I serve." Paul was not of this stripe, however. Far from feeling sorry for himself, he shared with them this blessed gospel. At their behest he walked up the stone steps to the top of Areopagus, the ancient judgment seat of Athens where in the crescent of stone seats had sat the judges who 300 years previously had condemned Socrates to die. Here this ambassador of the Judge of the earth delivered probably the greatest sermon ever to come from the lips of mortal man.

Thorough preparation was an essential characteristic of Paul's ministry. As soon as God had saved him in Damascus, he immediately started preparation in Arabia and then in Jerusalem, developing skill (consider this against the backdrop of the preceding chapter) in the work for which God had called him. He was speaking to the intellectuals of the world. The laws of this city pronounced death upon anyone introducing a foreign deity. Did that stop Paul? He was a Jewish tentmaker "whose bodily presence is weak and whose speech is of no account," but he spoke out in that classic and proud city of the ancient world.

It was in the marketplace at Athens that Socrates, "the wisest" of men, asked his immortal questions. Over in the nearby olive groves by the brook, Plato founded his academy. To the east was the Lyceum of Aristotle. Near at hand in the Agora were the garden of the Epicureans and the painted porch of the Stoics. Here was the home of the drama where the scholars spoke with pride the names of Aeschylus and Sophocles. Here spoke the orators of Greece. Here were historians like Thucydides and Xenaphon. In their Athenian temples the national spirit of Athens was deified in the marble images of their heroes and soldiers, in the trophies of her victories, in her multifarious objects of interest. Here Paul introduced a foreign deity—God Almighty.

Here Paul preached:

The personality of God
The self-existence of God
The omnipotence of God
The unity of God
The reality of divine providence
The universality of divine providence
The efficiency of divine providence
The spirituality of divine worship
The nonexternality of divine worship
The unity of the human race
The brotherhood of the human race
The possibility of a true natural religion
The dignity of man
The dependence of man
The absurdity of idols and idol worship
The essential graciousness of God's dealings with the race of man
The duty of immediate repentance
The certainty of a day of judgment
The exaltation of Jesus Christ to the office of supreme judge
The reality of a future life.

Here Paul corrected the errors of:

Atheism, or the dogma that there is no God
Pantheism, or the theory that all is God
Materialism, or the notion that the world is eternal
Fatalism, or the superstition that no intelligence presides over the universe, but all things come to pass either by necessity or chance
Polytheism, or the fancy that there are or can be many gods
Ritualism, or the imagination that God can be honored by purely external performances
Evolutionism, or the hypothesis that man is a product of force and of matter

Indifferentism, or the creed that man should seek after
 nothing and no one higher than himself
Optimism, or the delusion that this is the best possible
 world and man has no sin of which to repent
Unitarianism, or the tenet that Christ was an ordinary
 member of the race
Annihilationism, or the belief that after death there is
 nothing
Universalism, or the sentiment that all will be saved.

Talk about skill! Talk about mastering one's field! What
discipline!

The development of this skill required great industry,
and Paul had learned the wisdom of industry. He was always
engaged in some worthwhile pursuit. Because of his dili-
gence, God was pleased to open up to him doors of opportunity. As a result of the effective execution of his opportunity, God blessed his ministry and at the same time delivered him from fear and anxiety. "I know both how to be
abased and I know how to abound" (Philippians 4:12).

He was so busy he had no time for fear-producing, worry-
loaded thoughts!

Paul refused to worry even though he was imprisoned in
Rome. Read 2 Timothy 4:13. He makes request of Timothy to
bring the "books, but especially the parchments." Industry!
This mighty man of God remained industrious right to the
end.

Many people piously assert that they are bound "to wait
upon the Lord" and to "trust in the Lord" while they sit on
the stool of do-nothing, twiddle their thumbs, and piously
pretend to be waiting for the Lord's return. Now it is true that
we must "wait upon the Lord" and "trust in the Lord."
Nevertheless, the proof that we are waiting upon the Lord
and trusting in the Lord will be revealed in our "always
abounding in the work of the Lord" (1 Corinthians 15:58).

By industry I refer to activity with a worthwhile purpose
and toward a worthwhile goal. This is essential to the poise
that conquers worry since you cannot fasten your mind upon

two things at once. You cannot throw all your energies into God-glorifying activity while at the same time focusing your attention upon fear-producing thoughts.

Death is characterized by inaction, life by action. As death approaches, action decreases. It can also be proved that decreasing activity hastens death. Do you not know some people who were in good health until their retirement and then it seemed as though immediately their health began to break and death ran toward them like Mercury with wings at his heels?

There are some who would rationalize their idleness by their advanced years. Don't think to immunize yourself from the responsibility to industry simply because you are advanced in years.

Commodore Vanderbilt built most of his railroads when he was well over 70, making his hundreds of millions at an age when most men have retired.

Kant wrote some of his greatest philosophical works when he was past 70.

Goethe wrote the second part of *Faust* after he was 80 and Victor Hugo was still astounding the world with some of his finest writings after his eightieth birthday.

Tennyson was 83 when he wrote "Crossing the Bar."

Benjamin Franklin most helped his country after he was 60.

Palmerston was premier of England at 81, Gladstone at 83. Bismarck was vigorously administering the affairs of the German empire at 74. Christy was premier of Italy at 75.

Verdi wrote operas after he was 80.

Titian painted his incomparable "Battle of Lepanto" at 98, his "Last Supper" at 99.

Michelangelo was producing masterpieces in the field of sculpture at 89.

Monet was painting great masterpieces after 85.

I believe that one of the outstanding factors contributing to the longevity of Sir Winston Churchill and General Douglas MacArthur was the fact that they both knew and utilized the value of industry.

Men like these mentioned don't have time for anxiety. Worry is a time thief and they refuse to be robbed by it.

Norman Cousins, for years the celebrated editor of *Saturday Review*, believes there is a relationship between creativity and longevity. He illustrates his conviction with the experience he had in visiting two men who, at the time of his visits, were octogenarians—Pablo Casals and Albert Schweitzer. He tells about Pablo Casals just before his ninetieth birthday being assisted at about eight o'clock in the morning by his young wife, Marta, to the piano. Mr. Cousins said that watching Casals move, one was aware of his many infirmities—what appeared to be rheumatoid arthritis, emphysema, swollen hands, and clenched fingers. He was badly stooped, and his head pitched forward as he walked with a shuffle.

Then Mr. Cousins tells how Casals arranged himself at the piano and began to play the opening bars of Bach's *Wobltemperierte Klavier*. It appeared as though a miracle were taking place in front of Mr. Cousin's eyes. Casals' fingers slowly relaxed. His back straightened. He breathed more freely. He hummed as he played.

Then he plunged into a Brahm's concerto, and his fingers "now agile and powerful raced across the keyboard with dashing speed."

The older active octogenerarian, Albert Schweitzer, told Mr. Cousins, "I have no intention of dying so long as I can do things. And if I do things, there's no need to die. So I will live a long, long time." Schweitzer lived to be 95.

I concluded a long time ago that people who find joy in their work and who are committed to a life of productive industry enjoy the kind of poise conducive to good health and longevity. Furthermore, industry is consistent with God's will for each life.

19

Poise Through Stewardship

In talking about stewardship I am referring to material possessions, time, and talents.

No man has a right to expect blessings from God if he, through greed and covetousness, blocks the pathway down which God's blessings march.

God is the owner of all things. We are stewards. God knew that man would contest this fact and so He went to special pains to make His ownership clear in the opening chapters of the Bible. God's name is mentioned 14 times in the first 13 verses, 31 times in the first chapter, and 45 times in the first two chapters of Genesis.

God requires stewardship not because of His need, but rather because of our need. He has no need.

> For every beast of the forest is mine, and the cattle upon a thousand hills. . . . If I were hungry, I would not tell thee: for the world is mine, and the fulness thereof (Psalm 50:10,12).

> The silver is mine, and the gold is mine, saith the Lord of hosts (Haggai 2:8).

God has a threefold basis for demanding our stewardship. Read Isaiah 43:1:

> But now thus saith the Lord that created thee, O Jacob, and he that formed thee, O Israel, Fear not: for I have redeemed thee, I have called thee by thy name; thou art mine.

He created us, He redeemed us, and He sustains us. It is impossible for a man to experience the poise that conquers worry unless he possesses an awareness of the approval of God. Without the awareness of divine approval, man is plagued by feelings of guilt and consequent fears. He may be a Hottentot in Africa, or a man-eating savage from the South Sea Islands. He may be totally uncivilized; but as a result of that monitor God has placed in his breast, man knows that he is responsible to a higher power. Not until he comes to know this higher power—God Almighty—personally through the mediation of Jesus Christ is his guilt resolved and do his fears subside.

Many are foolishly trying to get victory over guilt and fear by the utilization of Freudian expressionism and catharsis, Gestalt formulas, positive thinking, and the like. However it is only God who banishes our fear and through the instrumentality of the Holy Spirit gives us the spirit "of power, and of love, and of a sound mind" (2 Timothy 1:7).

It is possible for a Christian to be out of fellowship with God and thus forfeit the poise that is dependent upon our awareness of His approval.

God has set forth certain principles which transcend the boundaries of time segments, geographical divisions, and race groups. One principle God set down was the principle regarding time which He made eloquently clear in the first chapter of the Bible: *One day out of seven belongs to Him.* This principle has never changed, though it has been disobeyed and denied and abused. God has never rescinded this requirement.

Another principle that transcends time is the principle regarding *the doctrine of substitutionary sacrifice as the only answer to man's sin.* When Abel offered an atoning sacrifice it was in response to this fundamental law—this unalterable principle. Hebrews 11:4 tells us that Abel offered the sacrifice "by faith," meaning that there had been a revelation from God concerning it. Now all sacrifices have had their fulfillment in Christ, "the Lamb of God which taketh away the sin of the world" (John 1:29).

The third fundamental law—unalterable principle—is that

relating to *the stewardship of material possessions.*

Attention! If you are inclined to get a little impatient with this emphasis on stewardship and turn over to the next chapter, I implore you to hear me out—or rather hear God's Word out. One out of every six verses of the four gospels has to do with the right and wrong use of material possessions and 16 of our Lord's 38 parables have to do with the right and wrong use of material possessions. Don't sin against yourself by ignoring this chapter. Suspend your judgment and "to thine own self be true." Surely more anxiety, worry, and divided-mindedness among Christians is caused by deficiency at this point than at any other.

In the Garden of Eden God kept to Himself the tree of knowledge of good and evil. This He did to remind Adam and Eve of their stewardship and of God's ownership. They were not to touch the fruit of that tree. It belonged to God in a special sense. True, everything belongs to God, but a certain proportion of that which He bestows upon us is to be set aside immediately and with no strings attached.

Is not the tenant farmer in the Midwest required to give back to the owner one-fourth of the corn crop? Is not the tenant farmer in the South required to give back to the landowner one-third of the cotton crop? Since God is the owner of all things, is it not fair that we be required to give back to Him a proportion of that which He makes possible?

Remember verse 5 of our text in Philippians 4. The word *moderation* means "fairness" among other things. There is no poise without fairness and there is no fairness without stewardship of material possessions. This poise that brings peace is significantly dependent upon our obedience to stewardship opportunities.

The most impelling incentive to give is not to provide the church with financial resources. The child of God *pays* his tithe and *gives* offerings over and above the tithe "as the Lord hath prospered him":

1. In recognition of God's sovereign ownership:

But thou shalt remember the Lord thy God: for it

is he that giveth thee power to get wealth, that he may establish his covenant which he sware unto thy fathers, as it is this day (Deuteronomy 8:18).

What? know ye not that your body is the temple of the Holy Ghost which is in you, which ye have of God, and ye are not your own? For ye are bought with a price: therefore glorify God in your body, and in your spirit, which are God's (1 Corinthians 6:19,20).

2. In appreciative acknowledgment of redeeming grace:

For by grace are ye saved through faith; and that not of yourselves: it is the gift of God:
Not of works, lest any man should boast.
For we are his workmanship, created in Christ Jesus unto *good works*, which God hath before ordained *that we should walk in them* (Ephesians 2:8-10).

3. In surrender of life and talents to the Lord:

I beseech you therefore, brethren, by the mercies of God, that ye present your bodies a living sacrifice, holy, acceptable unto God, which is your reasonable service. And be not conformed to this world; but be ye transformed by the renewing of your mind, that ye may prove what is that good, and acceptable, and perfect, will of God (Romans 12:1,2).

When you prepare your tithe, you prepare for worship. In church as you put the money in the collection plate you are saying in substance, "This is a tangible expression of my total surrender to Thee. This money that I place in this plate represents my brains, my blood, my abilities—all of the blessings that have come from Thee, for I realize that

Every good gift and every perfect gift is from

above, and cometh down from the Father of lights, with whom is no variableness, neither shadow of turning (James 1:17).

"It is because of the health, because of the mental ability, because of the friends, because of the various resources that Thou hast given me that I am able to make a living. All that I am and all that I have is Thine. My stewardship of material possessions is but an expression of that fact."

The basis of our monetary responsibility is the tithe. Tithing is paying back to God ten percent of the increase. God says that if you fail to pay that ten percent back into the "storehouse" with faithful regularity you are a thief and a robber.

There are those who would try to brainwash people into believing that the responsibility of the tithe was only in force during the days of the law—from the time of Moses to the time of Christ. They will tell you that Malachi 3:10 has no relevance for today because it is in the Old Testament. The Lord must have known that such mischief would be attended. Therefore He introduced the words of Malachi 3:6, "For I am the Lord, I change not. . . ." After these words He calls Israel back to His ordinances, to tithes and offerings, to the storehouse, and to His conditional promise of blessing. The New Testament reaffirms these words of Malachi 3:6 by saying that with God there is "no variableness, neither shadow of turning."

These same people who say that tithing was for those under the law turn to Psalm 23 for comfort, to Psalm 32 for guidance, to Job for wisdom and comfort in trials and tribulations, to Elijah for a pattern of prayer, and to other Old Testament passages for leadership.

To be consistent, these people who would throw out Malachi 3:10 ought also to throw out John 3:16 because it, too, was spoken prior to the time that redemption was completed by our Lord on the Cross of Calvary.

Tithing antedated the law. Abraham tithed. The law of the tithe is not an Israelite law. It is a fundamental and unalterable law of God. It is still in force. That is why tithing is commended by Jesus.

> Woe unto you, scribes and Pharisees, hypocrites: for *ye pay tithe* of mint and anise and cummin, and have omitted the weightier matters of the law, judgment, mercy, and faith: these ought ye to have done, and *not to leave the other undone* (Matthew 23:23).

Just as Abraham paid tithes to Melchizedek so we pay tithes to Christ. In Hebrews 7 this truth is made clear. The Son of God who liveth and abideth a priest continually after the order of Melchizedek "receiveth tithes"—receives them now! When paying tithes, Abraham acknowledged Melchizedek's sovereignty for he was a king-priest. Likewise today when one pays his tithe he acknowledges Christ as his Sovereign, his Lord. Refusal to pay the tithe is refusal to own Christ as Sovereign and as one's High Priest. Thus one makes Christ not only inferior to Melchizedek, but also inferior to the Levites, the priestly group of Old Testament times.

The tithe was incorporated in the law. This was done because it was a principle worthy of divine enforcement. God never repealed the fundamental law of tithing; grace has not annulled it; time has not altered it.

Tithing was commanded by Malachi.

> Will a man rob God? Yet ye have robbed me. But ye say, Wherein have we robbed thee? In tithes and offerings.
>
> Ye are cursed with a curse: for ye have robbed me, even this whole nation.
>
> Bring ye all the tithes into the storehouse, that there may be meat in mine house, and prove me now herewith, saith the Lord of hosts, if I will not open you the windows of heaven, and pour you out

a blessing, that there shall not be room enough to receive it.

And I will rebuke the devourer for your sakes, and he shall not destroy the fruits of your ground; neither shall your vine cast her fruit before the time in the field, saith the Lord of hosts.

And all nations shall call you blessed: for ye shall be a delightsome land, saith the Lord of hosts (Malachi 3:8-12).

In this command Malachi makes the practice of tithing essential to receiving blessings of a superior nature and to a degree and in a measure not otherwise promised.

This passage in Malachi teaches that when a man refuses to tithe he is: 1) guilty of robbing God, 2) subjected to a curse, and 3) denied the right of the blessings of God.

Grace does not abrogate the law. Grace fulfills the law—and goes much further than the most stringent demands of the law. Grace provides the dynamic necessary for fulfilling the law's mechanics. The law told man what to do, but failed to provide him with the capability to accomplish it. Grace provides the dynamic of the Holy Spirit whereby in the strength of God man fulfills the demands of the law—and much more.

Jesus said in Matthew 5:17-20:

Think not that I am come to destroy the law, or the prophets: I am not come to destroy, but to fulfill.

For verily I say unto you, Till heaven and earth pass, one jot or one title shall in no wise pass from the law, till all be fulfilled.

Whosoever therefore shall break one of these least commandments, and shall teach men so, he shall be called the least in the kingdom of heaven: but whosoever shall do and teach them, the same shall be called great in the kingdom of heaven.

For I say unto you, That except your righteousness shall exceed the righteousness of the scribes

and Pharisees, ye shall in no case enter into the
kingdom of heaven.

Already in this chapter it has been pointed out that Jesus
commended the tithing of the Pharisees. In verse 20 of Matthew 5, the Lord tells us that our righteousness must *exceed*
the righteousness of the scribes and Pharisees. Grace fulfills
and amplifies instead of destroying and minimizing the law.

Proceed further in Matthew 5. The law says, "Thou shalt
not kill." Jesus makes it clear that if a man hates his brother he
is just as guilty as if he had murdered him. The law said,
"Thou shalt not commit adultery." Jesus points out that under
grace whosoever looks on a woman to lust after her has
already violated the seventh commandment in his heart.

Carry this principle over in the matter of the stewardship of
money. How can an enlightened child of God do less under
grace than the Jew did under the law? The Jew gave offerings
over and above his tithe, too. For instance, if you will study
the Old Testament you will discover that the Temple and the
equipage thereof were paid for by offerings over and above
the tithes. There is always a question mark in my mind about
the person who goes to extremes to prove that we are under
no obligation to tithe. What is his motive?

In Leviticus 27:30 God makes it clear that "The tithe is the
Lord's." Therefore we, as stewards, have absolutely no right
to handle it as though it were ours. It must be placed where
God says and when God says. Namely, in the storehouse on
the Lord's day.

Jesus said, "Render therefore unto Caesar the things which
are Caesar's; and unto God the things that are God's" (Matthew 22:21).

In other words, pay your taxes and pay your tithes. Your
taxes belong to the government. The proof of this lies in the
fact that they are deducted from your pay before you receive
it. Your United States income tax is to be paid to the collector
of Internal Revenue at a given location.

Suppose you owed the government an income tax of a

thousand dollars. Suppose that you made out your 1040 Form and attached a note to it in which you said:

> Dear Uncle Sam,
>
> You will notice that I owe you a thousand dollars. I am sending $100 to my local postmaster. He is one of your faithful servants and he is having a hard time financially. I am sending $100 to a U.S.O. down in South Carolina. They are doing a magnificent work boosting the morale of your own servicemen and they need help desperately. I am sending $100 to a nephew of mine who is a sailor with the Seventh Fleet. He is liable to get blown up any time and I think that he needs encouragement. After all, he is one of your faithful servicemen. Then I am sending $200 to the Veterans Administration. After all, they are loyally dedicated to carrying out your will. *But*, Uncle Sam, just to let you know my heart is in the right place, I am sending the remaining $500 to the collector of Internal Revenue in my area here.

"Absurd," you say. Why? Simply because no man would survive this miscarriage of responsibility with impunity.

Here is a man who owes God a tithe of a thousand dollars. But instead of accepting God's revelation that "The tithe is the Lord's" he says "The tithe is mine. My tithe!" Then, acting on that premise he high-handedly determines the distribution of that money which is not his in the first place. He will send $100 to a radio evangelist, another $100 to a Bible school, and another $100 to a missionary. The tithe is to go into the storehouse, which in this age is the church. *All the tithe is to go into the storehouse.*

Hear the Word of the Lord:

> Upon the first day of the week let every one of you lay by him in store, as God hath prospered him,

that there be no gatherings when I come (1 Corinthians 16:2).

Bring ye all the tithes into the storehouse, that
there may be meat in mine house, and prove me
now herewith, saith the Lord of hosts, if I will not
open you the windows of heaven, and pour you out
a blessing, that there shall not be room enough to
receive it (Malachi 3:10).

The same word that is translated "store" in 1 Corinthians
16:2 is the word used in the Septuagint translation and translated "storehouse" in Malachi 3:10. In other words, it would
be a correct translation of 1 Corinthians 16:2 to say, "Upon the
first day of the week let every one of you lay by him in
storehouse . . ."

These scriptural truths are set forth by one who doesn't
pastor a local church. Rather, he leads up a para-church organization dependent upon the gifts of God's people.

Gifts over and above the tithe can be made to Christian
causes. But "the tithe is the Lord's." The specific depository is
the local church, and it is to be placed there undesignated.

In 1957, when the Lord led me to resign the pastorate to go
into the field of evangelism, a dear friend who fought this
truth said, "Haggai, now I reckon you will abandon this
foolishness about storehouse tithing."

"My change in ministry doesn't mean a change in Scripture or commitment," I replied.

"Follow that notion, and in a year you will collapse for lack
of support," he insisted.

Said I, "If this ministry is of God, He'll supply the need."

It was, and He has.

When a man refuses to storehouse tithe his money, he is
repeating in kind—if not in degree—the sin of Adam and Eve.
They took to themselves an authority that was not theirs in
partaking of the forbidden fruit. That tree belonged to God,
not to them. When a man does not tithe, he is taking to
himself an authority that is not his in appropriating to himself money that belongs to God. How then can he expect

peace? How can he expect victory over anxiety and freedom from worry? For God and God alone is the Author of peace.

Here is a man who will not honor God with the payment of the tithe. However, when his little child becomes critically ill, and the doctors say there is no hope apart from supernatural intervention, that same father will fall on his face before God and in substance will say, "O God, this is my child, bone of my bones, flesh of my flesh, blood of my blood. I hand him to Thee. Do what seems good in Thy sight. If it can please Thee, restore him to health and strength and to us." Such hypocrisy! He is willing to trust God with his own flesh and blood! Even this man who is not willing to trust God with his filthy silver and gold? Does he think more of his money than he does of his child? Do you see the hypocrisy of it, dear friend? How can God honor a man like this? How can God in justice bless a man like this who turns his back upon God when he so desires—yes, turns his back upon God every time he refuses to tithe.

Yet another illustration. You will remember the passage in Mark 12:41-44. Jesus sat over against the treasury and beheld how the people cast money into the treasury. You will remember, also, that a certain poor widow put in two mites. Jesus called His disciples together, and said, "This poor widow hath cast more in than all they which have cast into the treasury." How could He know? Perhaps they had put part of their tithe into a religious foundation, or some Bible college, or sent it to some radio evangelist. You say, they didn't have such things back then! That's true, but let me hasten to add, it is a fact of history that there were more depositories for the giving of alms in that day than there are today. The others could have said they had given much of the tithe to alms' depositories. Jesus judged their stewardship on the basis of what they put into the treasury of the house of God which today is our own literal, visible, local church.

Consider the process of bringing the tithe: 1)*Bring* the tithe. This couples tithing with worship. The two are inseparable. 2) Bring *all* the tithe. Don't deduct your doctor's bills,

your transportation to and from work, your insurance poli-
cies, your gifts to the Red Cross, United Appeal Drive, and so
forth. Bring a full 10 percent of your total increase. 3) Bring
ye all the tithe into the *storehouse*. When this is done your
responsibility ceases. Even when Paul was trying to get
money together for Jerusalem, he didn't tell the Corinthian
Christians to send their tithe there. He told them to put their
tithe in their local church and then he urged the church itself
to help out the church in Jerusalem.

Now notice the conditional promise of Malachi 3:10:

> And prove me now herewith, saith the Lord of
> hosts, if I will not open you the windows of heaven,
> and pour you out a blessing, that there shall not be
> room enough to receive it.

If I could not believe what God says about tithing, I could
not believe what He says about anything. Strange it is that
people will believe what He says about salvation, what He
says about heaven, what He says about hell, what He says
about baptism, what He says about soul-winning—yet they
will not believe what He says about tithing and the stewardship of possessions.

I know a wealthy man who has set up a religious foundation. He allegedly puts ten percent of his earnings into that
foundation and therefore considers himself a tither. However, he does not put the tithe where God says to put it. In
addition to that manifest disobedience, one of his corpora-
tions borrows the money that is in the nonprofit religious
foundation—borrows it at the rate of six percent. Therefore he
has access to money on which he has to pay no tax—money
that he uses to expand his business. You say, "Well, preacher,
God is blessing him." Is He? The trouble is that too many
people think only in terms of money when they think of
God's opening the windows of heaven and pouring out blessings.

I know a man who made $40 million last year, but because

of an ulcerated stomach he can't eat a decent piece of meat. There are some men who would give all of their money if they could buy peace of mind, the respect of their children, the love of their wife.

Once again, let me remind you that from a selfish standpoint it would be to my advantage to preach that a person has a right to place his tithe where he wants inasmuch as on that basis additional money could be secured to undergird the responsibilities of our team. However, I know that God would not bless it. Sometime ago a dear friend of mine suggested that a group of businessmen give $10,000 a year out of their tithes to undergird this ministry God has given me. I thanked him for his generous proposal but said quite frankly, "You are barking up a tree where was never found a possum. I would no more be a party to accepting a part of a tithe of you businessmen—a tithe which is not yours, but which is God's—than I would be a party to taking a portion of your income tax—tax which is not yours, but which is Uncle Sam's."

You say, "What does this have to do with worry?" Plenty! If you went downtown and stole $100 from a merchant, would you have peace of mind? No. You would probably think that people were talking about you every time they looked at you. You would feel uncomfortable when you got in the vicinity of the business owned by the merchant whom you abused and to whom you were indebted.

In the fourth chapter of Philippians from which textual basis of our formula for victory over worry is found, Paul mentions the liberality of the Philippians. Is it not interesting that the Philippian church was the only church in which Paul found no doctrinal or ethical error? Read the fourth chapter and notice how he commends them for their liberality in the matter of monetary stewardship. Many people glibly quote verse 19: "But my God shall supply all your need according to his riches in glory by Christ Jesus." But may I suggest that the fulfillment of that promise is conditional upon a spirit akin to that expressed by the Philippians and recorded in the immediately preceding verses?

One of the reasons that many people worry is financial adversity—an adversity sometimes begotten of their own stewardship disobedience.

> Honor the Lord with thy substance, and with the
> first-fruits of all thine increase: So shall thy barns be
> filled with plenty, and thy presses shall burst out
> with new wine (Proverbs 3:9,10).

He wrote those words under the inspiration of the Holy Spirit of God.

Failure to tithe is incontrovertible evidence that the guilty party is more interested in himself than he is in the work of the Lord. One of the chief causes of anxiety and worry is self-centeredness.

> Where your treasure is, there will your heart be
> also (Matthew 6:21).

When your chief concern is not merely how to tithe, but how to give offerings—generous offerings over and above the tithe to the glory of God—you will experience a joy and a peace the world cannot define.

When a man refuses to tithe, he does so either from ignorance or covetousness. God's Word states that covetousness is idolatry.

> Mortify therefore your members which are upon
> the earth; fornication, uncleanness, inordinate af-
> fection, evil concupiscence, and covetousness,
> which is idolatry (Colossians 3:5).

Money becomes a tin god. Men resemble their gods; they assimilate what they conceive to be desirable. With money as your god there is no peace. But if Christ is the Lord of your life, the dominant dynamic of your experience, the over-mastering passion of your interests, you inevitably begin to resemble Him who "is our peace" (Ephesians 2:14). As a result of your fellowship with Him, you begin to experience that peace that only He can give.

> Peace I leave with you, my peace I give unto you; not as the world giveth, give I unto you. Let not your heart be troubled, neither let it be afraid (John 14:27).

Avail yourself of the blessings (including poise) that God promises to those who honor Him with their substance.

20

Poise Through Surrender

> Neither yield ye your members as instruments of unrighteousness unto sin: but yield yourselves unto God, as those that are alive from the dead, and your members as instruments of righteousness unto God (Romans 6:13).

Hear the words of Paul once again:

> But what things were gain to me, those I counted loss for Christ. Yea doubtless, and I count all things but loss for the excellency of the knowledge of Christ Jesus my Lord: for whom I have suffered the loss of all things, and do count them but dung, that I may win Christ (Philippians 3:7,8).

To be sure, the person who has totally surrendered himself to Christ fulfills all the other contributory factors to poise that have been mentioned. It may seem as though some of these suggestions overlap, but I have put myself "on the stretch," as it were, to turn the diamond around and around at all angles so that light may be flashed from every facet of it.

Certainly you have been impressed time after time when you have listened to missionaries on furlough from a foreign field. You have been impressed by the fact that they have willingly forfeited economic affluence, wordly ease, the fellowship of relatives and friends here at home. They have a serenity, a poise, that bespeaks a peace which cannot be defined—"the peace of God that passeth all understanding" (Philippians 4:7).

After hearing a returned missionary from China, a young lady walked up to her and said, "I'd give the world to have your experience."

"That," said the missionary, "is exactly what it cost me."

> He that findeth his life shall lose it: and he that
> loseth his life for my sake shall find it (Matthew
> 10:39).

Many times while in the pastorate and even on occasions since entering the field of evangelism, I have been approached by people who said, in substance, "I know that if I yield my life to the Lord He is going to make me preach and I don't want to do it." With some it wasn't preaching, but some other sphere of service. There are people who apparently are plagued with the misconception that if they surrender themselves to the Lord He will require of them that which they do not want. This is a trick of the devil. When you surrender yourself to the Lord you will want what the Lord wants for you. God's Word says,

> Delight thyself also in the Lord; and he shall give
> thee the desires of thine heart (Psalm 37:4).

> If ye abide in me, and my words abide in you, ye
> shall ask what ye will, and it shall be done unto you
> (John 15:7).

God's Word tells us that if we, as human parents, give good gifts to our children, how much more will our Heavenly Father give good things unto them that ask Him! Now suppose my little son had come to his mother and me and said, in substance, "Mom and Dad, I want to do everything that will make you happy. I know that you have had much more experience than I, and there are many mistakes that I can avoid by following your counsel and advice. I beg of you to guide me and direct me. To the best of my ability I will follow your suggestions." Can you imagine my wife and me then going into another room and in a confidential conference saying, "Now little John Edmund has put himself completely in our hands and at our mercy. Therefore let us do everything we can to make him as awkward and miserable and frustrated as possible." That's absurd. If we would not treat our own son that way, how much more true it is that our Heavenly Father would not treat us that way.

> If ye then, being evil, know how to give good gifts unto your children, how much more shall your Father which is in heaven give good things to them that ask him? (Matthew 7:11).

> Like as a father pitieth his children, so the Lord pitieth them that fear him (Psalm 103:13).

With surrender comes poise that conquers worry.

Lot pitched his tent toward Sodom. Too bad. Lot was a child of God. Second Peter 2:7,8 makes that clear. But Lot went his way instead of God's way. As a result of his disobedience he lost—lost dearly. The Lord told him to get out of Sodom. His married daughters, his sons-in-law, and his grandchildren would not leave with him. Parents may take their children to Sodom, but rarely will they ever take their children out of Sodom once they have been in Sodom for any period of time. Lot lost his wife. She was turned into a pillar of salt. He lost all his possessions, his position in the city, his prestige. He lost the respect of his two married daughters who in a cave got him drunk and then committed incest with him whereby he became the father of one son by each of his own daughters. Oh, the grief, the anxiety that would have been spared had Lot only surrendered himself to the Lord. He was robbed of the "desires of his heart" because he refused to "delight himself in the Lord."

Some time ago, in a distant city, a mother came to me requesting an interview. She was greatly distraught mentally and emotionally. The anguish of her heart was torturing her body. She had been under psychiatric care for more than four-and-a-half years, during which time she had been subjected to shock treatments. She was a professing Christian and gave every evidence of sincerely wanting to do the will of God.

After some brief but pertinent probing I asked her quite frankly if there were something which had taken place in her life, whether years ago or more recently, that was constantly preying on her mind. She said there was. It was a sin committed during the days of adolescence. I asked her if she had confessed it to the Lord. She assured me that she had.

I said, "I imagine, from my observation, that you have confessed it over and over and over—probably a thousand times—to the Lord. Is that right?"

She shook her head affirmatively.

I said, "You see, actually, you are making God a liar. You confessed that sin once. God promised you absolute forgiveness as we read in the words of 1 John 1:9—'If we confess our sins, he is faithful and just to forgive us our sins, and to cleanse us from all unrighteousness.' "

I said, "The reason you are going through this torture is simply that you have not surrendered yourself completely to the Lord. You do not trust Him. You are not willing to take Him at His Word. He has forgiven you, but you refuse to believe it. You refuse to forgive yourself. You are making the mistake of thinking that repentance is repining and that self-examination is brooding. Now then, simply take God at His Word. Surrender your life completely to Him. Surrender the limitations of your finite mind to the assurance of His immutable word. He has forgiven you. Now in complete surrender—*believe it*."

I am happy to say there seems to be abundant evidence that the Lord has corrected the situation. She is now enjoying the poise that comes with surrender.

There are businessmen all over the nation who, petrified by fear and paralyzed by anxiety over reverses in their business, could enjoy business success and even more—the peace that passes all understanding—if they would only surrender themselves to God and take Him as their partner.

There are many homes internally divorced where husband and wife live together under protest in an atmosphere of tension simply because they refuse to surrender to Jesus

Christ. It is trite, but it is nevertheless true that "If their home were built upon the Rock, Christ Jesus, it would not be headed for the rocks of chaos."

Here then is the secret of poise—surrender to Christ. Remember:

I can do all things through Christ which strength-eneth me (Philippians 4:13).

He will strengthen us to observe the laws of self-control, relaxation, scheduling, stewardship, skill, industry, thought-control, and enthusiasm—all contributory factors in the mastery of poise which brings peace and conquers worry.

Part 4

PRAYER

21

Why Pray?

Paul's formula for victory over worry is Praise, Poise, and Prayer. Having discussed Praise and Poise, we now come to that leg of the tripod without which the other two legs of Praise and Poise cannot stand. That leg is prayer.

> Be careful for nothing; but in everything by prayer and supplication with thanksgiving let your requests be made known unto God (Philippians 4:6).

Peace is possible only to those who have related themselves to God through Christ—who is the Prince of Peace. The Bible declares:

> There is no peace, saith my God, to the wicked (Isaiah 57:21).

By "the wicked" is meant not only the guttersnipes, ne'er-do-wells, members of the riffraff of society. The wicked are those who, unrepentant of their sins, have either refused or neglected to come to the Son of God by faith. They have not received Him into their hearts.

Read very carefully, for what you are about to read is a staggering truth.

> And you hath he quickened, who were dead in trespasses and sins: Wherein in time past ye walked according to the course of this world, according to the prince of the power of the air, the spirit that now worketh in the children of disobedience (Ephesians 2:1,2).

God's Word here states that until you receive Jesus Christ
as your Savior and Lord, you are "dead in trespasses and
sins." As one who is dead in trespasses you are dead to God
and to every quality inherent in His nature.

What are these qualities? Some of them are holiness, righteousness, love, truth, wisdom, justice, and power. As one
who is dead to God you are therefore dead—and insensitive—
to holiness, righteousness, love, truth, wisdom, justice, and
power. Now pause just a moment and think what that means.
To be sure, those who are dead in sin and therefore dead to
God have set up standards. Unfortunately they are not God's
standards. "Every man is a law unto himself." That explains
marital discord, domestic strife, civil factiousness, labor-
management antagonism, national crime, and international
tensions.

As one dead in sin and therefore dead to God you are alive
to Satan and to the qualities inherent in his nature. Some of
these qualities are sin, hostility, error, folly, injustice, weakness, and fear. As a child of disobedience you are dominated
and controlled by him. Read it again. He is "the spirit that
now worketh in the children of disobedience."

Someone takes issue and says, "Well, I'm not a drunkard.
I'm not a murderer. I'm not a sex libertine. I'm not an extor-
tionist. I'm not a troublemaker. I'm not a thief. I'm not a
blasphemer." Of course not. It is not to Satan's interests that
everyone be a drunkard, a murderer, a sex libertine, an extor-
tionist, a troublemaker, a thief, or a blasphemer.

He transforms himself as an angel of philosophic light,
moral light, social-justice light, political light, and cultural
light.

Until you come to Jesus Christ as a self-confessed sinner
and by faith accept the salvation which He has provided, you
are spiritually dead. Death means separation. Physical death
means separation of the body from the personality. By per-
onality I refer to all of the unseen facets of man's being,
including soul, spirit, mind, and heart. Spiritual death is
separation of man in this life from God. Eternal death is the

irremediable and unalterable separation of the total man from God forever.

Now, because you are spiritually dead, you are separated from God. Therefore you have no peace. Nor can you have any peace. You can use the power of positive thinking, resort to Gestalt psychology, adhere to Freudian suggestions, but it all will be to no avail. Your only hope is in Christ, the Prince of Peace, through whom you have access to God.

Life is union just as death is separation. Physical life is the union of the body and the personality. Spiritual life is synonymous with spiritual life.

When you receive the Lord Jesus Christ as your Savior you do not receive simply a new concept or a new creed, or a new formula for living. You receive a Person. It is "Christ in you" (Colossians 1:27). You receive a new nature.

> Whereby are given unto us exceeding great and precious promises: that by these ye might be *partakers of the divine nature,* having escaped the corruption that is in the world through lust (2 Peter 1:4).

Eternal life is the life of God in the soul of the believer. For the child of God, that which we call physical death is but a transition from life to life more abundant, from time to eternity, from the finite into the infinite. Therefore when one receives spiritual life he receives in kind, though not in degree, right here and now, everything that he will enjoy in heaven: communion with God, the favor of God, victory over sin, a transcendent love, divine motivation, and *peace.*

As mentioned, the formula for peace—victory over worry—is Praise, Poise, and Prayer. No unbeliever can have this perfect peace. The prayer of the unrighteous is an abomination before God (Proverbs 28:9).

God will not hear those who persist in unbelief.

> If I regard iniquity in my heart, the Lord will not hear me (Psalm 66:18).

The only way anyone can come to God is through Jesus
Christ.

> Jesus saith unto him, I am the way, the truth, and
> the life: no man cometh unto the Father, but by me
> (John 14:6).

The blind man whom Christ healed in John 9 stated the
truth—a truth that is refuted nowhere in God's Word—when
he said:

> Now we know that God heareth not sinners; but
> if any man be a worshipper of God, and doeth his
> will, him he heareth (John 9:31).

Prayer is a family matter—a matter between God the Father,
and born-again believers, His children.

Worry is a weakness of the flesh. You cannot conquer a
weakness of the flesh in the energy of the flesh. It must be
done in the power of God. Prayer gives you access to that
power.

Prayer is fundamental because it makes available to you the
divine dynamic whereby you master the mechanics leading to
victory over worry. Prayer is essential to Praise. Prayer is
essential to Poise. God shows us what we must do for victory.
In response to prayer He channels to us through the indwell-
ing Holy Spirit the ability to do what we ought to do—which
is to obey His commandments.

Prayer raises us to God's level. It takes us into God's atmosphere. It brings us into communion and intimacy with God.

Prayer signifies dependence upon God. Without Him we can do
nothing. With Him we can do everything. He is the source of
our strength.

> I can do all things through Christ which strength-
> eneth me (Philippians 4:13).

He is the source of our resources.

But my God shall supply all your need according
to his riches in glory by Christ Jesus (Philippians
4:19).

The Grecian says, "Man, know thyself." The Roman says,
"Man, rule thyself." The Chinese says, "Man, improve thyself." The Buddhist says, "Man, annihilate thyself." The
Brahman says, "Man, submerge thyself in the universal sum
of all." The Muslim says, "Man, submit thyself." The twentieth-century internationalist says, "Man, learn the art and
practice the principles of peaceful coexistence." But Christ
says, *"Without me you can do nothing"* (John 15:5).

Conversely, with Him we can do anything.

Prayer is the means whereby we make contact with God's
strength and in Him overcome our weakness.

Only when we set aside our own strength will the Lord
really become our strength.

Attempt to float. As long as you exercise your own efforts to
keep up you will go down. Give yourself up to the water and it
will immediately sweep under you with its waves and bear
you up in its strength.

The Lord Himself is our strength. Don't pray, "Lord, give
me strength," as though you are asking Him for a quality
distinct from Himself. Rather say, "O Lord, be Thou my
strength."

Listen to Ephesians 3:20:

Now unto him that is able to do exceeding abun-
dantly above all that we ask or think, according to
the power that worketh in us.

Here again you have that word *energeo*. And the word
translated power is the word *dunamis* from which we get the
word *dynamic*. Just as Satan and his "powers of darkness"
energize the unbeliever, so God energizes the obedient Christian. He becomes the divine dynamic whereby the believer
conquers all things—including worry.

The same power that burnishes each star, points each blade
of grass, hurls each wave upon the shore, formed the body of

our Savior, raised Jesus from the dead, and will raise our bodies or transfigure them in the hour of glory, is the same power which is available to each obedient Christian. This power is made available through prayer.

This power is available only to those who are weak. God's helpfulness is meted out only to those who confess their helplessness.

And he said unto me, My grace is sufficient for thee: for my strength is made perfect in weakness. Most gladly therefore will I rather glory in my infirmities, that the power of Christ may rest upon me. Therefore I take pleasure in infirmities, in reproaches, in necessities, in persecutions, in distresses for Christ's sake: for when I am weak, then am I strong (2 Corinthians 12:9,10).

Our strength lies in childlike helplessness. In your helplessness through prayer, cast yourself upon Him who is our strength. The very essence of the meaning of prayer is that you need help beyond your own strength.

The reason many of us do not pray is that we are too strong—strong in our own false, swaggering, blustering strength. We are strong in our own strength, the very heart of which is utter helplessness, emptiness, and weakness.

Worry is an intrusion into God's province. You are making yourself the father of the household instead of the child. You are setting yourself up as the master of God's kingdom, instead of the servant for whom the Master provides.

The basis of prayer is man's need and God's ability to meet that need. When one really prays he is confessing his utter helplessness. He is casting himself completely and wholly upon God. He is delighting himself in the Lord. Consequently the Lord grants unto him the desires of his heart.

Our needs are manifold. Our perplexities are multifarious and variegated. Don't worry. Instead, turn your care into a prayer. Follow the example of Paul who said, "I conferred not with flesh and blood" (Galatians 1:16). Conferring with flesh and blood about your worries instead of taking them to God is a fruitful cause for increased worry.

Years ago, while I was still in the pastorate, I concluded a Sunday night service with the benediction. Even before the choir's response had ended, an anxious woman rushed up to me and asked if I would talk with her child who was under conviction of sin and wanted to be saved.

It was my joy to see that keen and energetic youngster enter into peace with God through Christ. We had prayer together. As I rose to dismiss them, I realized that the mother was in agony, and she looked at me as if to say, "I am in such trouble. Can you help me?"

I asked her if she would like to speak with me. She grabbed the opportunity as a drowning man would grab a life belt. I asked the youngster to step into the next office for just a moment. Turning to the mother I said, "All right. Would you like to share with me the problem that is causing you this grief?" She burst into uncontrollable sobs. I assured her that having been pastor of a church of over three thousand members for several years I was now shockproof. I further reminded her that everything would be in strictest confidence.

Let me stop here long enough to tell you that this lady was one of the outstanding members of the church. She taught a Sunday school class, was prominent in the Training Union and in the Women's Missionary Society. She almost never missed a service. She tithed her money. She knew her Bible. If Gallup had taken a poll of the membership, I am sure this lady would have ranked among the most respected of all members.

Finally, she blurted out her story. I sat transfixed with astonishment as she told the most sordid story of duplicity and sin I ever had heard from a supposedly respectable woman.

Finally she nearly screamed out, "Preacher, have I committed the unpardonable sin?" It was my joy to assure her from God's Word that if she still desired to repent, God would receive her. I assured her in the words of Jesus who said, ". . . him that cometh to me I will in no wise cast out" (John 6:37b).

For 11 years she had been trying to win in her own strength the battle of life. Though not yet 40 she had already aged considerably. Her health was poor. She was under psychiatric care. Finally she came to Christ.

Today she is a charming, radiant Christian. Her health is fine. Her mind is free from personality-corroding, body-debilitating, mind-destroying worry.

It wasn't until she confessed her helplessness and cast herself wholly upon God that she received strength to live dynamically. Now, as a child of God, she has a prayer life by which she maintains communion with God and keeps unclogged the channel through which His strength is released to her moment by moment and day by day.

Pray because prayer is essential to poise. Recall the story of Daniel in the lions' den. You remember that he had been hounded by the men who were bent upon his destruction. Nevertheless, he did not alter his habit one iota. There was no ruffling of his spirit. He continued to make his prayer unto God three times a day. He prayed in a spirit of deep humility, recognizing his absolute dependence upon God. Was this a sign of weakness? No! It was a sign of strength. To be sure, Daniel put his face in the dust before God, but he did not lose his courage before the wrath of Darius. He sobbed like a heartbroken child when he knelt before his God, but he faced without a quiver the jaws of the hungry lions. What poise!

There is a real efficiency in prayer. This fact ought also to induce a greater interest in prayer. Martin Luther was not talking through his hat when he said, "I have so much business I cannot get along without spending three hours daily in prayer." Prayer is efficient in that it saves time. It saves time by conditioning you for the day's activities and personal contacts. It saves time by conditioning those with whom you will associate. It saves time in that it makes available to you wisdom which in turn leads to quick and proper decisions.

> If any of you lack wisdom, let him ask of God,
> that giveth to all men liberally, and upbraideth not;
> and it shall be given him (James 1:5).

This of course leads to peace of mind. How many people there are who fret and mope around wasting precious time simply because they don't know what to do or how to do what they need to do. The Lord has promised them the needed wisdom, but they either refuse it or neglect to avail themselves of it. The resultant loss of peace and time is incalculable.

Let me digress here for just a moment. In chapter 23 stress is given to the importance of definite periods of prayer and waiting upon the Lord in prayer. You have just read the words of James 1:5. How ridiculous it is for the Christian to ask for wisdom and immediately terminate his prayer, taking leave of Him who is the Source of wisdom before He has had time to impart it. What would you think of a man who walked into your home and with apparent earnestness asked you a question, but turned around and walked out before you had time to answer it? Remember, prayer is not a one-way street. It is a two-way street.

Prayer is efficient because it puts you in touch with *infinite intelligence*. Prayer will dispel the fogs of human ignorance. It banishes the darkness of self-destructive errors in judgment. People of prayer, regardless of their academic limitations, are the recipients of a proper perspective and a keen understanding imparted to them by Him who is "the Truth."

Prayer is efficient in that it makes available to you the grace necessary to block out negative thoughts, distracting attitudes, and worries which torture the mind and deteriorate the body. Through prayer we cast

> . . . down imaginations, and every high thing that exalteth itself against the knowledge of God, and bringing into captivity every thought to the obedience of Christ (2 Corinthians 10:5).

When your thoughts are Christ's, they are not worry thoughts.

Prayer is efficient in that it enlists divine strength enabling you to effect the proper execution of your God-given responsibilities. While in the flesh upon this earth our Lord prayed before every great endeavor.

Prayer is efficient in that it can lead to the correction of circumstances that both consume time and saddle a person with destructive grief. Do you remember the prayer of Moses and Aaron on behalf of their sister Miriam who was suffering with leprosy? How would that story have ended had it not been for their prayer?

Prayer is efficient in that it leads to harmony. Read once again the first chapters of the Acts of the Apostles. How differently history would have been written had it not been for the prayer of the 120 in the upper room. The harmony that prevailed between them was one of the by-products of their prayer lives. We read concerning them, "and all that believed were together, and had all things common" (Acts 2:44). Worry cannot survive in an atmosphere of such harmony.

Prayer is efficient because it is productive of faith. And faith, of course, is the antidote to worry. Faith is acting in confidence upon the word of another. The one who is faithful in his prayer life acts in confidence upon God's Word. He goes to God with all his dilemmas, all of his assets and all of his liabilities. He acts in confidence upon God's Word which tells him that if he delights himself in the Lord, the Lord will give him the desires of his heart. He prays. God answers his prayer. The very answer is productive of greater faith—of a more eager and a more earnest disposition to act in confidence upon God's Word.

Prayer is efficient because it leads to inner security. The person who spends time regularly in prayer comes to know in his inmost soul that God's Word is true when He assures us, ". . . I will never leave thee, nor forsake thee" (Hebrews 13:5). The resulting inner assurance leads to much greater efficiency.

For instance, I know a man who always insisted on picking up the tab at the restaurant every time he and his friends were eating out. If he went to a ball game with ten or fifteen other folks, he insisted on paying the bill. He constantly gave away expensive gifts—gifts he simply could not afford. Why? His dreadful insecurity is the only answer I can conceive. He compensated for the lack of inner security in his mad effort to secure the fervent friendship of a host of people whose gracious responses to his generosity gave him a temporary sense of well-being.

When a man is properly related to God he has within himself all of the ingredients necessary to provide him with security, joy, and peace regardless of external conditions. This relationship is only maintained as a man spends time regularly with God.

Why pray? Pray because prayer is the means whereby you permit and invite God to so energize you that to His glory you live victoriously, overcoming the world, the flesh, and the devil.

Yes, pray because through prayer you enlist the power of the spirit of God to conquer the weakness of the flesh—*even worry*. When your thoughts are Christ's, they are not worry thoughts.

Pray, because through prayer you have opportunity to turn every care into a prayer.

22

How to Pray

Once again,

> Be careful for nothing; but in every thing by prayer and supplication with thanksgiving let your requests be made known unto God (Philippians 4:6).

In this verse, three different Greek words for prayer are introduced. The first word, translated "prayer," refers to a general offering up of wishes and desires to God. This word points to the frame of mind required in the petitioner—a mind of devotion. The word refers to unrestricted concourse between man and God. That which brings greatest glory to God and profit to you is the habit of prayer. We might call it the Prayer Mood or the Prayer Disposition.

The word translated "supplication" comes from a Greek word meaning "entreaty," a "seeking," "need," "indigence." It refers to an entreaty impelled by a great sense of need, an extreme want. In fact, the verb form of this word in the original means "to want." Therefore this word refers distinctly to the petitionary prayers that are expressive of personal need. This prayer is a special petition for the supply of wants, an act of solicitation.

The third word used and translated in the King James, "requests," refers to requests and even more strongly to demands.

Now the word translated in the King James as "prayer," includes adoration, thanksgiving, confession, and intercession.

The word translated "supplication" refers strictly to an entreaty to God to supply our needs and our wants. On the basis of the teaching of Philippians 4:6 it would be well for us to ponder several factors involved in effectual praying.

If you would have victory over worry, pray *intelligently.* "Let your requests be made known unto God." I heard of a certain man who spent six hours in prayer each day. Lest he should go to sleep when on board a boat, he stood upright and had a rope stretched across, so that he might lie against it. If he slept he would fall. His object was to keep on for six hours with what he called prayer. What sort of prayer was it? He kept on repeating, "There is no God, but God. There is no God, but God." He repeated the same thing over and over again. He did not plead with God to give him anything. Just as a witch repeats a charm, so he repeated certain words. That is not praying.

If you go on your knees and simply repeat a certain formula, you are speaking only words. You are not praying. Some people are criticized for using beads and fetishes to "say prayers." But there are many Protestants who just as definitely "say prayers." They do not pray. They repeat formulas. They say prayers as did the farmer who each night prayed, "O Lord, bless me, my wife, my son John, his wife, us four, no more. Amen." God does not hear you for your much speaking.

Even though on Mount Carmel the wild-eyed multitude cut themselves and chanted repetitiously, "O Baal, hear us!" they were not praying. Let your *requests* be made known unto God.

Get alone with God and tell Him what you want. Pour out your heart before Him. He does not care for high-flown language. Study the prayers of the Bible and you will be impressed that there was no formal phraseology, and there was no fixed and mechanical use of words. Go to God as you go to your mother, your father, or your friend.

Don't think that simply because you get on your knees for a spell every morning and every night that God is going to dissipate your worries. Pray intelligently. Tell Him your problem. Tell Him that you have sinned—that you have worried. Tell Him that you want victory over it. Be specific.

And that leads me to say if you would have victory over worry, pray *definitely*. In chapters 1 and 3 you learned what worry does to you physically. You also learned that worry is a sin. Therefore, as a worrier, you have a great need. Offer up supplications to the Lord—"entreaties expressive of your personal need that solicit God's answer for that need."

Indefinite praying is usually halfhearted praying. Indefinite praying is often insincere praying. It is usually a mere formality. There is no burden, no urgency, no overwhelming constraint in indefinite praying. Indefinite praying shows that one is not sure of the will of God. Therefore he knows not what to pray for. It often indicates that one is trusting in the *act* of praying rather than in the God who answers prayer.

The mind of man is so constituted that it cannot fasten its desires *intensely* upon numerous things at the same time. Jesus said,

> Therefore I say unto you, What things soever ye
> desire, when ye pray, believe that ye receive them,
> and ye shall have them (Mark 11:24).

Now it is impossible to desire strongly that which is not definite.

Your problem is worry. Pray definitely about this problem. Pray definitely that God will give you victory over your distrust of Him. Pray that God will forgive you for intruding into His own province by trying to carry on His business. Ask Him for the grace to cast all your cares upon Him.

In addition to all this, pray specifically concerning the problems causing your anxiety. If it is a wayward daughter, pray definitely and specifically for God's will to be done in her life and for God to give you the grace in the meantime to live triumphantly.

If it is financial difficulty, pray definitely that God will show you if you have been unwise in the handling of your money. If you have been unwise, ask Him to forgive you. Pray definitely that He will give you wisdom and grace to do what you can. Pray that He will miraculously do what you can't do.

Then rest in the truth of Psalm 37:25, "I have been young, and now am old; yet have I not seen the righteous forsaken, nor his seed begging bread."

If you are suffering from a nervous stomach pray definitely about it. Don't simply say, "Lord, take away my nervous stomach." Find out what are the causes of your condition. Be specific. Be definite. And then let your request be made known unto God. Or, as we could correctly translate it, "Make known your demands."

Every now and then I hear people say, "God heard my prayer, but He answered it a little differently than I was expecting." That is ridiculous. What would you think of me if I had five sons and I prayed, "Lord, save my five sons." A few days later my neighbor's five sons all went to church and professed faith in Jesus Christ. Supposing that I said, "Praise God; He answered my prayer. I prayed for the salvation of my five sons and He answered my prayer. He saved the five sons of my next-door neighbor." That is nonsense.

Pray definitely and expect a definite answer. Pray for bread. God will give you bread, not a stone. Pray for fish. God will give you a fish, not a serpent.

If you would have victory over worry, pray *importunately*. The word *importunate* means both "demanding" and "persistent." These qualities are consistent with the text. Remember, the word *requests* can be translated "demands." The tense used is the present imperative so that we might translate the words this way—"in everything by general concourse with God and specific entreaties arising out of peronal needs, with thanksgiving, let your demands be made known *perpetually* unto God."

You can make these demands because of your relationship with God through Christ. "But my God shall supply all your need according to his riches in glory by Christ Jesus" (Philippians 4:19).

He has promised to supply all your needs. You can demand the fulfillment of that promise with this warning, however. You are not to say, "Lord, supply all of my needs." Rather you

are to specifically and definitely make known those needs
one by one. And then pray persistently. Your cares are persistent. Therefore make your prayers persistent.

Pray to God and then pray again. If the Lord does not
answer you the first time, be grateful that you have good
reason for praying again. If He does not answer your requests
the second time, thank Him that He loves you so much that
He wants to hear your voice again. If He keeps you waiting
until you have gone to Him seven times, say to yourself,
"Now I know that I worship the God of Elijah, for Elijah's God
let him go again seven times before the blessing was given."

Count it an honor to be permitted to wrestle in prayer even
as Jacob wrestled with the angel during the long watches of
the night. This is the way God develops His princes.

Jacob never would have been "Israel"—Prince with God—
if he had received the blessing from the angel at the first
asking. He kept on wrestling until he prevailed. Then he
became a prince of God. Worry cannot exist with this kind of
prayer.

Jesus taught us to pray all the way through the gospels.
Two great illustrations He gave to us in the eleventh and in
the eighteenth chapters of Luke.

The man who wanted to borrow bread at midnight is a
striking example of the spirit Jesus desires to inculcate. The
borrower was in dire need. He was terribly in earnest and
would not take no for an answer. Jesus said when you pray be
just as earnest and be just as persistent as this man was. You
need the blessing of God much more than he needed his three
loaves. You are seeking something that means more than
bread, and just as the importunity of the borrower finally
wins out, so the soul set upon finding God will command His
attention and be heard.

God has no time for lukewarm pleas, for easygoing, half-
hearted prayers. If the sense of need is not great, if you forget
about the matter before the day is over, God will pay little
heed to your prayer. If you have something vital at issue, if
you are willing to give time and effort, and if you press your

claim home to a finish, God will listen. The man who is willing to quit, or who can quit, is not in the condition of mind and heart to appreciate the favor of God. The soul who counts it the biggest privilege on earth to know God, who seeks for Him and His blessings as men seek for silver and gold, will not only be rewarded, but also will be conditioned to estimate rightly what has been received.

Jesus then adds:

> And I say unto you, Ask, and it shall be given you; seek, and ye shall find; knock, and it shall be opened unto you. For every one that asketh receiveth; and he that seeketh findeth; and to him that knocketh it shall be opened (Luke 11:9,10).

This is not the easy passage some people think it is. It does not mean that all you have to do is ask for something and receive it, or to knock and the door flies open. It refers to a life which is one continual search after God, a constant seeking, a daily asking, a habitual knocking.

This is the only antidote to worry which itself is perpetual. Let your prayer be perpetual. It means that you must desire that which lies behind the closed door intensely enough to knock with unshaken persistence. Jesus is here saying that to such knocking the door will open. To seeking of that sort will come the answer which makes life full and rich.

The parable found in the eighteenth chapter of Luke is still more striking, as it represents a case where the delayed answer is misunderstood. The petitioner is set forth in the figure of a poor widow seeking vindication and protection from an unjust judge. The judge is the perfect embodiment of heartless wickedness. No more complete portrait of utter depravity was ever drawn than Jesus sketched in that one terse sentence, "which feared not God, neither regarded man" (Luke 18:2). Just one stroke of the Master Artist's brush, and the cold, heartless man stands before us; one who regards not suffering humanity nor fears the coming judgment of God.

The feeble, insignificant petitioner was scorned. No heed was given, but Jesus said she continued to press her plea for justice until in absolute selfishness and for no other reason the judge granted the request.

> . . . Though I fear not God, nor regard man; Yet because this widow troubleth me, I will avenge her, lest by her continual coming she weary me (Luke 18:4b,5).

The argument is: If a man like that can be moved to do what means nothing to him, will not God hear the continual cry of His people He loves with a boundless compassion? There are long periods when prayers seem unanswered. There are long days of darkness, sometimes years of wearisome waiting, while countless petitions are sent to a heaven that seems deaf and empty. This is the time about which Jesus speaks. He says, "Cry on, God will hear. He is not heartless, neither has He forgotten."

This parable is for the time when faith has staggered and the heart has grown sick with waiting. Let us remember that the longest delay to us may be as the twinkling of an eye to the plans of God. Alexander Maclaren said years ago, "Heaven's clock does not beat in the same note with our little chronometers." Jesus teaches us to pray on. He says we must not quit. We must not doubt. God knows when to answer. He knows the best time and the most fitting place. We can, in all confidence, leave the question of *when* and *where* to Him. Of one thing we may be sure—*He will answer*. Worthy prayer does not become discouraged. It does not surrender. This is the power that defeats worry.

If you would conquer worry, *pray in faith*. Faith is acting in confidence upon the word of another. Faith in God is acting in confidence upon His Word. You were saved that way. It is also in this way you become mighty with God.

You develop faith as you meditate upon God's Word—the Bible.

> So then faith cometh by hearing, and hearing by

the word of God (Romans 10:17).

Prayer and the Word of God are inseparably connected. "Feasting" on the Word of God is productive of that faith without which prayer is useless.

Through the Word of God the Lord speaks to our hearts and conditions our hearts for prayer. In prayer we speak to Him in faith. So many times in the Scriptures we have passages indicating that the Lord spoke first, after which the one who heard the Word of the Lord spoke to Him in prayer. Read Jeremiah 1:4-6 as an example.

> Then the word of the Lord came unto me, saying, Before I formed thee in the belly I knew thee; and before thou camest forth out of the womb I sanctified thee, and I ordained thee a prophet unto the nations. Then said I, Ah, Lord God! behold, I cannot speak: for I am a child.

You remember also Daniel's great prayer. In the first year of the reign of King Darius we see Daniel reading the Word of God. He had in his hand the prophecy of Jeremiah in which the Lord had promised that the desolation of Jerusalem should last 70 years. After reading this prophetic promise, Daniel turned to the Lord. The reading of the Word of God led to prayer. The reading of God's Word was productive of the faith that made prayer effectual.

The German theologian Bengel had the reputation of being a great man of prayer, one who knew the secret of effectual prayer. One day a fellow believer watched him at the close of the day. He saw the old saint sitting before a large Bible, reading slowly, often stopping, meditating with the silent tears running down his cheeks. After reading and meditating a long time, Bengel closed the Book and began to speak to God in prayer. His heart had been prepared through the reading of the Word. Neglect of the daily reading of the Word of God and meditation on it soon results in neglected prayer as well.

The secret to earnest and effectual prayer—the prayer of faith—is faithful and diligent study of the Scriptures.

Faith is essential to effectual prayer. All real prayer has as its basis a firm faith in a God who reponds to the quest of the human soul.

> But without faith it is impossible to please him:
> for he that cometh to God must believe that he is,
> and that he is a rewarder of them that diligently seek
> him (Hebrews 11:6).

We come to God by our hearts and not by our intellects. The first condition of entering into His fellowship is a faith not only that God is, but that He will be found by the soul who honestly and persistently seeks for Him. God is not found by those who look for Him in the spirit of cold curiosity. He is not found by those who simply desire to extend the range of their intellectual conquest. This is the reason why many self-styled philosophers and many pseudoscientists have been unable to come to any clear conception of God. It was to men of this type that Zophar said,

> Canst thou by searching find out God? canst
> thou find out the Almighty unto perfection? (Job
> 11:7).

When a man says in the pride of his intellect, "I will now see if there be any God," he may turn his telescope upon the farthest heavens and count the myriad worlds that wander in the blue abyss. He may peer among the atoms and divide and subdivide the electrons, but the greatest thing in the universe will still be hidden from his eyes.

The laws of logic, the theories of philosophy, the investigation of chemistry and physics, all have their place and are of great value, but they are not milestones on the road into fellowship with God. The man who can say with the Hebrew psalmist, "My soul thirsteth for God, for the living God: when shall I come and appear before God?" (Psalm 42:2), is more nearly on the road to His presence. The humble man who with simple and sincere faith reaches out after God will find Him while the philosopher is groping in the shadows of his theories and the scientist is bewildered with the problems of his laboratory.

If you would enter into the prayer life that conquers care, spend some time each day with the Word of God. The time spent will be productive of faith that pleases God. This time spent will condition you for communion with God and as you commune with God you will develop ever more confidence in God and this glorious cycle will continue unabated as long as life shall last.

You worry. Here is God's Word that if you will utilize this formula of Praise, Poise, and Prayer He will give you peace. He also makes it clear that by prayer you will be given strength to offer praise and to manifest poise. As you pray you will become effective in prayer. Now believe this. Believe that He will give you precisely what He has promised to give you if you will meet the conditions. He will give you *peace*.

He cannot go back upon His promise. He is "the God, that cannot lie" (Titus 1:2).

Some of you pray, but you only say words. While you are asking God to give you victory over worry, you are at the very time worrying that you are not praying correctly. You are worrying that maybe you have not met all of the conditions. *Stop psychoanalyzing yourself.* Don't be a spiritual hypochondriac. *Get your mind off yourself and onto God. Spend enough time in your prayer thanking Him for what He has done and praising Him for who He is that you will be conditioned to pray intelligently, definitely, importunately, and in faith.*

As you pray, picture yourself a perfectly adjusted, dynamic, radiant personality living in the strength of God to the glory of God. This is certainly God's will for you. By faith, then, take God at His Word, lay hold upon Him in prayer, and become the personality to glorify Him and bring peace to your mind. You are what you think you are. Stop, therefore, insulting God. Recognize yourself as a redeemed soul. You

are a child of the King. You are in league with the Creator of
the universe. Recognize yourself as a potential recipient of
qualities, attitudes, and resources that will glorify God and
bless your fellowman as you live triumphantly over every
worry and care.

If you would conquer worry, pray *privately*.

> But thou, when thou prayest, enter into thy
> closet, and when thou hast shut thy door, pray to
> thy Father which is in secret; and thy Father which
> seeth in secret shall reward thee openly (Matthew
> 6:6).

God deals with men face to face and heart to heart. You
cannot have audience with a king and be engaged with the
crowd at the same time. The matters between you and God
are too sacred and personal to be laid bare to the eyes of the
crowd. Furthermore, prayer calls for such concentration,
such focalization, such rallying of all of our powers, that it
demands the quiet of the inner chamber. When we pray we
are going to share with God things which we would not for
the very life of us share with the crowd. There are the secrets
of our hearts to be talked over with Him. There are sins that
need to be confessed to Him. There are yearnings and hun-
gerings of our deepest souls to whisper into His ear about
which we would not for anything speak to our dearest friend.
Then God wants a real opportunity to speak to us. "The still,
small voice" cannot be heard amidst jarring sounds, shattering voices, the hum of machinery, or the clamor of business.

Jesus did not mean that no man could pray unless in an
empty and quiet room. He did mean that the door of mind
and heart would shut out the world. The outside world must
be locked away from the private transactions which take place
there. "When thou hast shut thy door," when there is no one
there but God and you, when you are all alone with Him,
then pray.

It is so true that when we really pray, no one is there but
God and ourselves. All else is outside. When we pray, our

dearest earthly friend is outside the door. He may be in the same pew, in the same room, but he is outside the door. Every business affair is without. Every allurement of the world is without. All the silver that shines and the jewels that sparkle are outside the locked door when we really pray. Not a distraction, not an alien sound! How quiet it must be in there! One can almost hear the beating of his own heart and the rustle of his thoughts. That door is not made of steel or lumber. It is the door of our will that closes and says to all the world, "Out. Out. Out. I have great business at hand! I am engaged with the Almighty. Keep out!"

I tell you, worry cannot abide when you are locked up with God in the secret sanctuary of prayer.

If you would conquer worry, pray *thankfully*. This will lead your mind to revert back to chapter 6 where the text says that we are to pray and supplicate "with thanksgiving." The kind of prayer that kills worry is a prayer that asks cheerfully, joyfully, thankfully.

Pray, "Lord, I am in financial straits. I bless Thee for this condition, and I ask Thee to supply all my needs." This is the way to pray. "Lord, I am sick. I thank Thee for this affliction for Thou hast promised that 'all things work together for good to them that love the Lord.' Now heal me, I beseech Thee—if it please Thee!" Or you will pray, "Lord, I am in great trouble. I thank Thee for this trouble for I know that it contains a blessing even though the envelope is black-edged. Now, Lord, give me grace as I pass through this trouble." This kind of prayer kills worry.

If you would conquer worry, pray in *Jesus' name*.

If ye shall ask any thing in my name, I will do it (John 14:14).

And in that day ye shall ask me nothing. Verily, verily, I say unto you, Whatsoever ye shall ask the Father in my name, he will give it you. Hitherto have ye asked nothing in my name: ask, and ye shall receive, that your joy may be full. These things have I spoken unto you in proverbs: but the time cometh, when I shall no more speak unto you in proverbs, but I shall shew you plainly of the Father. At that day ye shall ask in my name: and I say not unto you, that I will pray the Father for you: For the Father himself loveth you, because ye have loved me, and have believed that I came out from God (John 16:23-27).

Years ago I was involved in a four-car accident. Litigation proceedings began almost immediately. I needed help desperately. I needed the resources of the greatest accident lawyer in the country. His name was Weinstein. His fee was understandably large. So large that I, as a ministerial student, could not meet its demands. However, a dear friend of mine hearing of my need, came to see me. This friend was part owner of a large company in Chicago. He said, "Haggai, Weinstein is our lawyer. We retain him. Here, let me give you one of my cards." On the back of the card he scribbled a note of introduction to Weinstein. Weinstein saw me. He solved my legal problem. Why? Because of a fee I paid? Not at all. Because of the fee paid by my friend. He received me in the name of and on the merits of my friend.

The Lord Jesus Christ is my Friend "that sticketh closer than a brother." He paid the fee that I could not pay—the penalty of sin. He paid it with His own blood. In His name and on His merits I have access to God who alone can solve my problems.

Catch this insight. Grasp this concept. And you will be well on the way to the conquest of worry.

23

When to Pray

The tense used in Philippians 4:6 is present imperative. It carries the idea of durative action. Therefore we are being true to the meaning of the text when we translate Philippians 4:6, "Don't worry about anything whatever, but in all things by prayer and supplication with thanksgiving, let your requests be made known *perpetually* to God."

The present imperative tense is also used in the first part of the verse. In other words, Paul is saying, "Don't perpetually worry, but *perpetually* pray." *Let perpetual prayer take the place of perpetual care.*

Prayer is the Christian's breath. When breathing is obstructed, health is jeopardized. When the Christian permits any obstruction to his prayer life, his spiritual health is put in jeopardy.

Our little son breathed only once every two and a half minutes the first three hours he was in this world. Because of his deficient breathing only an inadequate supply of oxygen could reach the brain with the result that brain tissues were destroyed and body movement was impaired. Many Christians are suffering from spiritual cerebral palsy. An inadequate supply of the oxygen of prayer has destroyed spiritual fiber and impaired Christian effectiveness.

Breath is essential to life and health. The breath of prayer is essential to Christian well-being. When the Christian is praying, he is breathing spiritually. Just as we must breathe ceaselessly, so we must pray ceaselessly.

The injunction of God's Word is that we "Pray without ceasing" (1 Thessalonians 5:17).

The trouble with many of us is that we pray when caught in the swirl of difficulty, oppression, and vicious circumstances. Then we think of Psalm 50:15:

> . . . call upon me in the day of trouble: I will
> deliver thee, and thou shalt glorify me.

The story is told of two Irishmen, Pat and Mike, who had narrowly escaped death on a sinking ship. They were floundering around in icy ocean waters on a couple of planks. Pat was addicted to the grossest profanity but he decided to repent of it if the Lord would come to his rescue. Mike thought his theology sound. Pat assumed the countenance of a Muslim at Mecca and began to pray. Just before arriving at the main thesis of his repentant prayer, Mike spotted a ship coming toward them. As delighted as Columbus when he first spotted the North American shore, Mike hollered, "Hold it, Pat. Don't commit yourself. Here's a ship." Pat immediately stopped praying! Isn't that the way many of us are? The only time we pray is when we are in a jam. As soon as things improve we forget God.

Spiritually speaking, most of us can much better afford adversity than prosperity. Like the Israelites of old, it seems that when our prosperity expands, our spirituality contracts. Like Mike, we call upon the Lord as long as things are precarious, but as soon as things improve we resort to our own resources. The Lord is but an escape mechanism for some.

The Christian's prayer life is one of incessant prayer. "Praying always," says Paul in Ephesians 6:18. That is, praying at all seasons and on all occasions. If you would conquer worry, you must always maintain a spirit of prayer. You must live in a prayerful disposition.

"Pray without ceasing." One of my theological professors, in discussing the meaning of 1 Thessalonians 5:17, told of an experience of some ministers. They had congregated early and were waiting for the Monday morning ministers' meeting. They were talking in the vestibule and this verse was mentioned. Discussion became spirited and the meaning of this verse evoked no small comment—and consternation. It wasn't long until they readily agreed that the verse puzzled them. How could one possibly pray without ceasing? A scrub woman about her work overheard them and said, "Excuse me, gentlemen. But it's all very simple." She then gave her interpretation of the verse in the form of a personal illustration.

She said, "I always pray. When I go to bed at night I thank the Lord for the joy of resting on His everlasting arms. When I awaken the next morning I ask Him to open my eyes that I may behold new and wondrous things out of His Word. When I bathe I ask Him to cleanse me from secret faults. When I dress I ask Him to clothe me with humility and love. When building the fire I ask Him to build the fire of love for souls in my heart. When I eat I ask Him to cause me to grow on the bread of His Word." On and on she continued explaining to those ministers the way in which she lived in the attitude of prayer. Prayer was her habit. They marveled. They grasped the truth. We are to "pray without ceasing."

In praying without ceasing, one's mind is stayed on Christ. One is constantly attuned to the will of God. While one may not be involved in deliberate and conscious contact with Him, one is nevertheless aware of His presence and one's life is regulated by His will. It is much the same as a mother who goes to sleep at night. The little baby is in the crib. The mother is sleeping. Even while sleeping, however, she is attuned to the baby's needs and wants. The slightest whimper of the baby arouses her from sleep. So it is in the life of the Christian who prays without ceasing. He is attuned to the will of God. God's slightest suggestion, command, or desire arouses the believer to obedience and action.

Isaiah says: "Thou wilt keep him in perfect peace, whose mind is stayed on thee: because he trusteth in thee" (Isaiah 26:3). When you pray without ceasing, you are "attuned" to God. When you live in an awareness of His will, your mind is "stayed" on Him. Now the truth is simply this: When your mind is stayed on Him, you have perfect peace. When you have perfect peace you don't have worry. If you would conquer worry, it is essential that you live in the atmosphere of prayer.

The pages of God's Word are replete with the names of those who prayed. All who had power with God and with men were people of prayer. Explain the poise of Daniel in the lions' den apart from the mighty prayer life he maintained.

Moses prayed until his face glistened with the glory of God.

The great example, of course, is our Lord. His whole life was a prayer. Before He did anything He prayed. After He did anything He prayed. He prayed morning, noon, and night. Sometimes He prayed all night. Whenever He was alone He prayed. Prayer was never off His lips and was never out of His heart. He was the incarnation of this truth, "Pray without ceasing."

Let me caution you against a prevalent mistake. There are those who say, "I always pray. When I am driving the car down the street I pray. When I go about my business I pray. I never spend great periods of time alone with God in prayer. I simply pray all the time in whatever I do." This is well and good. But it is also essential that one set apart a period each day when he can get alone with God and pray.

Charles Simeon devoted four hours each morning to prayer. Mr. Wesley spent two hours daily in prayer. It is said that John Fletcher stained the walls with the breath of his prayers. Sometimes he would pray all night. His whole life was a life of prayer. Said he, "I would not rise from my seat without lifting my heart to God."

Martin Luther said, "If I fail to spend three hours in prayer each morning, the devil gets the victory through the day. I have so much business I cannot get along without spending three hours daily in prayer." David Brainerd, the mighty missionary to the Indians, once said, "I love to be alone in my cottage where I can spend much time in prayer."

Adoniram Judson said, "Arrange thy affairs, if possible, so that thou canst leisurely devote two hours every day, not merely to devotional exercise, but to the very act of secret prayer and communion with God . . . to be resolute in His cause. Make all practical sacrifices to maintain it."

You may not have hours to devote to prayer. D. L. Moody never spent more than 15 minutes in prayer. But he prayed *often* and *about everything*. It is important that you have a definite time when you get alone with God every day. Not everyone can spend great periods of time. But surely there are few people, if any, who could not spend at least ten to 15 minutes in Bible study and 15 minutes in prayer daily.

Let me urge you to begin the day with your quiet time. I find that the more I commit myself to the Lord in the morning the less I have to confess to Him at night. We need food to strengthen us for the physical demands of our daily routine. Matthew 4:4 and 1 Peter 2:2 indicate that the Word of God is spiritual food.

> . . . It is written, Man shall not live by bread alone, but by every word that proceedeth out of the mouth of God (Matthew 4:4).

> As newborn babes, desire the sincere milk of the word, that ye may grow thereby (1 Peter 2:2).

If you would be strong, you must have spiritual food at the beginning of the day to sustain you through it. You are not likely to suffer great temptations while you are sleeping. The great strains and stresses will be encountered during the day. Of course it is well to spend some time with the Lord before going to bed at night. But let me urgently suggest that you make your personal devotions a matter of first concern in the morning. An old professor of mine had the motto, "No Bible, no breakfast. Speak to no one until you have spoken to God."

The effectiveness of your brief moments of prayer will be contingent upon these periods spent in prayer. Don't say you have no time. Some may have more money than others. Some may have more talent than others. But we are all on an even footing when it comes to time. We each have 60 seconds to each minute, 60 minutes to each hour, 24 hours to each day, seven days to each week, 52 weeks to each year.

As an evangelist, I was gone from home a great deal. There were occasions when on my way from one city to another, I could stop at my home for a few minutes. It delighted my heart, and my wife and son gave evidence that this delight was reciprocated. Suppose, however, that when I had a week off between meetings, I refused to go home. Suppose I had gone off to visit some friends instead. The next time I "bounced in" I would probably have "bounced out" just as fast. My family knew that I loved to be at home and that I spent every possible moment at home. This knowledge made even the briefest visits enjoyable to all of us.

So, too, our brief visits with the Lord bring mutual rejoicing if we are faithful in setting aside larger segments of time to commune with Him in deliberate and earnest intercession. Then "would our hearts condemn us not."

When to pray? Let us once again paraphrase Philippians 4:6, and hear—"Let your requests be made known *perpetually* unto God."

Remember, perpetual prayer is the answer to perpetual care.

24

For What to Pray

Be careful for nothing; but in *everything* by prayer and supplication with thanksgiving let your requests be made known unto God (Philippians 4:6).

Casting all your care upon him; for he careth for you (1 Peter 5:7).

Since you worry about everything, pray about everything. "In *everything* by prayer and supplication with thanksgiving let your requests be made known unto God." Peter tells us to cast *all* our care upon Him. Turn *every* care into a prayer.

You may pray about the smallest thing and about the greatest thing. Set no boundaries with respect to God's care. It is a wide-open field. You may pray for the fullness of the Holy Spirit. You may also pray for a new pair of shoes. Go to God about the food you eat, the water you drink, the clothing you wear.

Nothing is too small for Him to notice. Does He not attend the funeral of every sparrow? Has He not numbered the hairs of your head? Even the things you might consider big are little, yet important, to Him. Our entire earth is like a mere speck of sand on the beach of the great universe. If God is willing to consider this little speck, He would just as well stoop a little lower and consider our smallest problems.

You worry about the smallest things, do you not? Well, pray about the smallest things, since prayer is God's antidote to worry.

Read it again: "Casting *all* your care upon him, for he careth for you." The words translated *care* here are two distinct and different words in the original. The word *care* used in the first instance is the same word translated "anxious." It refers to the same word relating to worry, "to divide the mind." The

word *care* used in the second instance refers to God's solicitous interest in our highest good. Cast *all* your mind dividers,
mind distracters, worries on Him for He is solicitous of your
highest good. Cast them *all* on Him.

You know the old song by Tindley, "Take Your Burden to
the Lord and Leave It There." The chorus goes,

> Leave it there, leave it there.
> Take your burden to the Lord and leave it there.
> If you trust and never doubt,
> He will surely lead you out.
> Take your burden to the Lord and leave it there.

The trouble with us is we pretend to take our burdens to the
Lord, but we don't leave them with Him. We bring them back
again.

Close friends of our family were living in Darlington,
Maryland, in the early '40's. The husband and father was a
classmate of my father during their school days. They had
eight children. The mother, whom we affectionately called
"Aunt Edith," was coming home from a neighbor's house one
Saturday afternoon. As she came nearer she saw five of her
youngest children huddled together in great concentration of
interest and effort. As she came near, all the time trying to
discover the center of attraction, she was aghast to see them
playing with baby skunks. She screamed at the top of her
voice, "Children, run!" *Each one grabbed a skunk and ran!* Isn't
that what we often do? We have our little worries, our little
problems—our little skunks. We take them to the Lord in
prayer. He says, "Run." Instead of leaving them there, we
grab the stinking little things and run.

No problem that I as a Christian have is too great or too
insignificant for God's loving care. This is a thrilling thought
that you will do well to ponder again and again.

A. T. Pierson, Bible teacher extraordinary, sat one day with
George Muëller, the great Englishman of faith. Mr. Muëller
was relating to Dr. Pierson some of the marvelous things God
had done for the Faith Orphanage at Bristol. As Mr. Muëller

talked he wrote, and Dr. Pierson noticed he was having difficulty with his pen point. In the midst of the conversation, Mr. Muëller seemed oblivious to the visitor. He bowed his head for a moment or two in prayer and then began writing again. Dr. Pierson said, "Mr. Muëller, what were you praying about just now?"

"Oh," said Mr. Muëller, "perhaps you didn't notice that I was having trouble with this pen point. I haven't another and this is an important letter, so I was asking the Lord to help me so that I could write it clearly."

"Dear me," said Dr. Pierson, "a man who trusts God for millions of pounds also prays about a scratchy pen point."

If Mr. Muëller had been like many of us, he would have become hot and bothered. Possibly he would have become a little exasperated with the man who sold him the pen or the company that made the pen. Perhaps he would have indulged in morbid reflection wondering why he didn't buy a pen of another make instead of the miserable pen that was giving him trouble. Or, if he had been like many of us, he may have in disgust thrown the pen down and discontinued the writing of the letter, with the result that his conscience would have bothered him later on for not having written. This would have added to the stress and anxiety. I draw your attention to this because I think it is one of the most lucid examples of the power of prayer in the seeming trivia of life.

Some there are who think we should pray only for problems of great magnitude. They consider it an insult to God and a waste of His time to pray for the so-called small things. It is here that we need the faith of a little child.

One day, many years ago, my father was replacing a burned-out bulb in the taillight of our old car. In replacing the lens he noticed he had lost a little screw in the tall grass. He had an urgent appointment for that night and not much time to spare. He searched and searched for the little screw, but to no avail. My younger brother Tom, then five or six years old, was playing next door with a friend. Finally, Dad called Tom and his friend over to contribute their help in finding the insignificant but essential little screw. When Dad told the children what he wanted Tom said, "Dad, have you prayed about it?"

My father replied, "No, I haven't, Tom."

Tom said, "Well, let's pray, Daddy." Tom prayed and said in substance, "Heavenly Father, Daddy has lost the screw that he needs for the taillight of his car. He can't find it and he needs it badly. Help us to find it. Thank You, Jesus. Amen."

Believe it or not, as soon as Tom had finished his prayer—so illustrative of the childlike faith that honors God—Dad put his hand down in the tall grass and retrieved the screw. Coincidence? Not at all! It was a distinct answer to prayer.

Possibly you read some years ago the article in *Reader's Digest* telling about the circumstances leading to Billy Graham's going on the air coast to coast. Many people had been after him to secure a coast-to-coast weekly broadcast. He had hesitated, saying that there were many other fine coast-to-coast broadcasts of the gospel. Also the finances were not available.

An increasing number of people insisted that for the glory of God and the profit of the people of America individually, as well as for America as a nation, it was imperative that Billy go on the air. Did Graham fret and stew and worry about whether or not he ought to go on? Did he let the decision upset him and thus reduce his effectiveness for Christ? Did he vacillate between the two possibilities? No. He simply took the issue to God in prayer.

Without publicizing the fact he put out a fleece as did Gideon. He prayed that if the Lord was leading him to broadcast the gospel coast-to-coast each week He would provide $25,000 within a specified time. As I recall, by the morning of the final day a little more than $23,000 had come in. Dr. Graham had set $25,000 as the figure. Did the fact that $25,000 in full had not come in upset him? Did he say, "Well, this is close enough"? Did he say, "My prayer is answered"? No. He had made his appeal to the Lord. He was honestly trying to know the will of God. His whole interest was the glory of God. If $24,995 had come in, Dr. Graham would not have

gone on the radio. Before the day was over, however, the full
$25,000 had come in and he knew the direction in which God
was leading him.

Some of you say, "But really, some of the things that come
to my mind are too insignificant to pray about." Do you really
believe that? If you believe they are too insignificant to pray
about, then why do you not believe they are too insignificant
to worry about? Put this down: Anything big enough to
worry about is big enough for you to pray about. Philippians
4:6 tells us in substance, "Don't worry about *anything* whatever; but in *everything* let your requests be made known unto
God."

In this book is set down the biblical formula for victory over
worry. If you are to have victory in putting this formula in
operation, it is mandatory that you enlist the strength of
Almighty God.

In your prayer ask God for the grace to enable you to
rejoice, to control your feelings, regulating them according to
His will, to count your many blessings. Ask Him to give you
grace to respond to ingratitude with serenity. Call upon Him
for the grace of becoming genuinely interested in other people.

By prayer call upon God to help you live in the consciousness of His nearness and therefore to display that poise which
is the hallmark of the domination of the infinite God in the
life of finite man.

Through prayer ask God to give you grace to "gird up the
loins of your mind" so that you might have the mind of
Christ.

> Let this mind be in you, which was also in Christ
> Jesus (Philippians 2:5).

Through prayer you will enlist divine help in the matter of
self-control, in the matter of relaxation (resting in the Lord),
in the matter of enthusiasm, in the matter of scheduling your
day's activities, in the matter of your hobbies and sidelines, in
the matter of living each day to the full by "redeeming the
time," in the matter of the development of skill, in the matter
of industry.

Through prayer spend time with God until you know His mind and do His will in the all-important matter of stewardship. Through the right kind of prayer life you will be strengthened to live the surrendered life so essential to the poise which conquers worry.

Through prayer you can duplicate the request of earnest men many years ago who, turning to Jesus said, "Teach us to pray."

The direct answers of God in response to your prayer give you strength to battle and conquer this vicious sin of worry. Apart from the blessings of prayer itself there is also a therapeutic value in the actual time and quiet spent before God.

Pray about everything. Turn every care into a prayer and *win over worry*.

Part 5

PEACE

25

Perfect Peace

> And the peace of God, which passeth all understanding, shall keep your hearts and minds through Christ Jesus (Philippians 4:7).

Ponder my translation of verse 7:

> If you do this, then the peace of God, far more effective than any forethought or contrivance of man will keep watch over your hearts and your thoughts in Christ Jesus.

The word translated "peace" can also be translated "tranquility," "harmony," "concord," "security," "safety," "prosperity," and "felicity." Worry cannot survive in this kind of atmosphere. Just as worry means "divide the mind," so we might say that peace is "uniting the mind," fastening it upon worthwhile goals and stimulating it with worthwhile motives.

God is the Author of this peace. It is "the peace of God." And God is not the Author of confusion.

> For God is not the author of confusion, but of peace, as in all churches of the saints (1 Corinthians 14:33).

He is the Author of unity.

> Endeavoring to keep the unity of the Spirit in the bond of peace (Ephesians 4:3).

This is a genuine peace begotten of God. This is not the attitude of the man who takes everything lightly—who snaps his fingers, whistles, and sings. This fellow is a heedless, foolish, light-headed, and light-heeled person who for a little while may dance and sing. He simply postpones his sorrow. The day will come when he will give account. The day will come swiftly and with a vengeance.

This peace is far different than that attitude and disposition embraced by the stoic. The stoic braces his nerves. He will be shaken and moved by nothing. Run a knife into him. He feels the pain, but he will not show it. Despite all manner of rough knocks and blows in the rough and tumble world, he has set his teeth, and no expression will escape him to show that he feels or winces. This is not peace.

This peace is far different from that attitude and disposition embraced by the laughing epicurean who chortles out, "Let us eat, drink, and be merry for tomorrow we die." We are not steel-nerved stoics. We will live it up.

This peace is based upon fact. It is not a self-manufactured hallucination designed to color the facts. This peace is based upon the fact of God's all-sufficiency. It is also based upon our willingness to cast ourselves in self-confessed helplessness upon Him in response to which He lives through us His own life, bringing harmony, purpose, meaning, and poise to our lives.

Let me make a distinction between *peace with God* and the peace of God. Every child of God has peace with God.

> Therefore being justified by faith, we have peace with God through our Lord Jesus Christ (Romans 5:1).

But not every child of God has the peace of God. No one can enjoy the peace *of* God who does not have peace *with* God. On the other hand, it is possible, as witnessed by the experience of multitudes of Christians, to have peace *with* God and fail to appropriate the peace *of* God.

This peace *of* God has its foundation in the fact that God doeth all things well. It has its source in the fact that Jesus "will never leave thee nor forsake thee" (Hebrews 13:5).

Do you remember the story in Mark 4 of our Lord's trip across the Sea of Galilee? He was asleep in the bottom of the boat. The winds became furious. The waves sprang higher and higher in the air. Soon a tempestuous storm was raging. The little boat was perched perilously aloft the crest one moment only to be dashed into the darksome vortex the next. The terrified disciples cried out, "Lord, save us. We perish!" Jesus was asleep! What peace.

Jesus arose and subdued the storm, and then turned to the disciples and said, "Oh, ye of little faith. Why are ye so fearful?" I can hear them muttering "Little faith? Little faith? We are veteran seamen. We have never seen a storm like this, and you call it little faith!" Ah, yes. You see, Jesus didn't say, "Let us go out in the middle of the sea and get drowned." He said, "Let us pass over unto the other side" (Mark 4:25).

Now, dear friend, when you have invited Christ into your life and when you have turned the helm over to His control and when you have heard His words of assurance, "Thou art mine, I will never leave thee, nor forsake thee" (Hebrews 13:5), there is made available to you a peace the world cannot give and the world cannot take away.

Notice several points about the peace Christ can give:

1) *It is a peace that "passeth all understanding."* This may be interpreted in two ways.

First, it may be interpreted as too great for the poor grasp of our limited concepts. It is deeper, broader, sweeter, and more heavenly than the joyful Christian himself can explain. He enjoys what he cannot understand.

There is another sense in which the words *passeth all understanding* refer to superiority over human forethought or intellectual contrivance. Here is a man who has worries. He tries through the efforts of his own understanding to resolve his worries. He fails. He fails miserably. He may resort to stoicism or epicureanism or the power of positive thinking, but he fails.

This man comes to God's Word. He responds affirmatively to God's commands. Having entered into peace *with* God he now utilizes that formula which gives the peace of God: **Praise** plus **Poise** plus **Prayer** equals **Peace**. Perfect peace is his privileged possession. In this sense it passes understand ing, in that it far exceeds in effectiveness all human contriv- ance and forethought.

2) *This peace is indestructible.* It "shall keep your hearts and minds through Christ Jesus." Paul here brings into union the conceptions of peace and of war, for he employs a distinctly military word to express the office of this divine peace. That word, translated "shall keep," is the same as the word trans- lated in another of his letters, "kept . . . with a garrison" (2 Corinthians 11:32).

This peace of God takes upon itself militaristic functions. It garrisons the heart and mind. By *heart and mind* are not meant two different faculties, the emotional and the intellectual. Here, as is always the case in God's Word, *heart* means the whole inner man whether considered as thinking, willing, purposing, or effectuating any other inward and volitional functions. The word *mind* does not mean another part of man's nature. Rather it refers to the total products of the operations of the heart. The revised version renders it "thoughts" and that is correct if it be made to include emo- tions, affections, and purposes as well as thoughts in the more restricted sense. The peace of God garrisons and guards the whole man in the full scope of his manifold operations. This divine peace can be enjoyed in the midst of warfare.

This is an indestructible peace that guards and garrisons one against all care, anxiety, change, suffering, and conflict. It gives unalterable rest in God.

Deep in the bosom of the ocean beneath the region where winds howl and billows break there is calm, but the calm is not stagnation. Each drop in the fathomless abyss may be raised to the surface by the power of the sunbeams, expanded there by their heat, and sent on some beneficent mission across the world. Even so, deep in our hearts beneath the storm, beneath the raging winds and the lashing waves, this peace forms a central calm, a calm that is not stagnation.

"Drops" of this calm may be raised to the surface of our behavior by the power of the Son of Righteousness—Jesus Christ, the Light of the World—expanded there by the heat of the Holy Spirit and sent on beneficent service across the world.

3) *This peace is perpetual.* The tense used here is future indicative and the context makes it clear that it is the progressive future which means continuous and unabated action.

Stop perpetually worrying. Perpetually let your requests be made known unto God. And you have the assurance that perpetual peace will garrison and guard your mind and heart through Christ Jesus. What an antidote to worry!

The assurance of this peace is conditional upon no outside circumstance, for this peace is possible only through Christ. A life without Christ is the life without peace. Without Him you have excitement, worldly success, fulfilled dreams, fun, gratified passions, but never peace!

Mr. Horatio G. Spafford was a successful lawyer in Chicago and a member of the Fullerton Avenue Presbyterian Church in that city. In the financial crisis of 1873, he lost most of his property. In the stress and strain of the times, he prevailed on his wife and four daughters to take a trip to France—to get as far away from the scene of worry as possible. He booked passage for them on the *Ville de Havre.* They set sail November 15, 1873.

The trip was uneventful, and its hundreds of passengers were enjoying the indescribable uplift of an ocean voyage. That is, until the night of November 22.

Shortly after midnight the *Loch Earn*, bound for New York, collided with the *Ville de Havre*. In a few minutes, the French ocean liner sank beneath the waves. The *Loch Earn*, which was not damaged by the collision, rescued as many survivors as they could find. Of the 226 passengers on the *Ville de Havre*, only 87 survived.

Mrs. Spafford was among the survivors, but the four daughters perished. As soon as Mrs. Spafford reached land, she telegraphed from France to her husband: "Saved alone. Children lost. What shall I do?"

The Chicago attorney left immediately to join his wife and bring her back to Chicago. It was in the depths of their bereavement that he wrote his one and only hymn, "It Is Well With My Soul." The grief of his terrible loss and the peace he experienced as he and his wife submitted their lives to God's providential dealings, he describes in the four stanzas of the hymn.

Perhaps the words will take on new meaning for you as you ponder them:

When peace, like a river, attendeth my way,
When sorrow like sea billows roll;
Whatever my lot,
Thou hast taught me to say,
"It is well, it is well with my soul."

Though Satan should buffet, though trials
should come,
Let this blest assurance control;
That Christ has regarded my helpless estate,
And hath shed His own blood for my soul.

My sin—oh, the bliss of this glorious thought,
My sin not in part, but the whole
Is nailed to the cross and I bear it no more,
Praise the Lord, praise the Lord, oh my soul!

And, Lord, haste the day when the faith shall be
sight,
The clouds be rolled back as a scroll;
The trump shall resound and the Lord shall
descend,
"Even so," it is well with my soul.

Christian friend, before you were saved you had no peace, did you? The Christless heart is like a troubled sea that cannot rest. There is no peace for it.

Now you are a Christian. The Lord has brought you peace with respect to your relationship with Himself and with respect to your outlook on eternity. However, if you are to enjoy the peace of God over daily worries and cares and anxieties, small though they be—"the little foxes spoil the vines"—you must fix your mind upon Him. "Looking unto Jesus" (Hebrews 12:2).

Keep your mind "stayed" on Him. This will enable you to fulfill the Bible formula of Praise, Poise, and Prayer.

Here is the glorious conclusion:

Praise plus **Poise** plus **Prayer**
equals **Perfect Peace**!

As Christ lives in you "your peace shall be as a river, and your righteousness as the waves of the sea."

Peace be with you.

Other Books by John Haggai

How to Win Over Pain
How to Win Over Fear
New Hope for Planet Earth
The Steward
My Son Johnny
Lead On!

About the Author

His home is Atlanta, Georgia. But his international influence touches millions of people because his field of operation is the world. His journeys have taken him around the world more than 60 times, and he travels over 200,000 miles every year. Dr. John Haggai, truly a world personality, is founder and president of Haggai Institute for Advanced Leadership Training headquartered in Singapore.

John Haggai was born in Louisville, Kentucky, the son of an immigrant to the United States who fled his native Syria during Turkey's harassment of Syria in 1912.

A prolific writer, Dr. Haggai's first book, *How to Win Over Worry*, has been a bestseller since 1959 and is now published in over 15 languages. This was followed by *New Hope for Planet Earth, How to Win Over Loneliness, My Son Johnny,* and *The Steward.* Dr. Haggai credits many of the concepts he has developed in his books to his long-term friendship with Paul Meyer. (Mr. Meyer is a member of the Board of Directors of Haggai Institute.)

Because of his reputation as an informative and captivating speaker, Dr. Haggai has been sought after by a variety of audiences. These include the world's largest Rotary Club; the Kiwanis International Convention; the Institute for Human Development in Seoul, Korea; the Texas Medical Association; international investment bankers on Wall Street; graduate students at Yale University; the Texas Academy of Family Practice; as well as numerous other civic clubs, colleges, and universities on all six continents.

John Haggai's face and his name suggest his East-West ethnic ancestry. To the people of Asia he looks like an Asian, not a Westerner. But it's more than a matter of looks or a name . . . he has an empathy for the people of Asia.

OTHER GOOD HARVEST HOUSE READING

BLOW AWAY THE BLACK CLOUDS
by *Florence Littauer*

Florence Littauer helps the reader to come to terms with the emotional handicap of depression, offers practical insight on how to determine the cause—physical, psychological, or spiritual—and maps out the guidelines for constructive action to overcome depression.

BOUNCING BACK
Finding Acceptance in the Face of Rejection
by *William Coleman*

Rejection is coming, just like bad weather! How we cope with its devastating effects will mean the difference between success and failure in our lives. Best-selling author William Coleman explores with sensitivity and insight such topics as: types of rejection, preparing your children to handle rejection, self-rejection, bouncing back when you feel you can't. Coleman's compassionate approach and godly counsel will help you turn the hurt of rejection into building blocks for a healthy self-image.

FREEDOM FROM GUILT
by *Bruce Narramore* and *Bill Counts*

Silent condemnation cripples and enslaves many sensitive Christians. But there is freedom from both depression and fear of failure. The authors combine their insights to illuminate the path of complete forgiveness and self-acceptance.

HOW TO WIN OVER FEAR
by *John Haggai*

Fear is a pervasive and destructive influence in modern society. Everyone seems to be afraid of something. Dr. John Haggai explores the different types of fears, the essential prerequisites and formula for winning over fear, and God's power that is available to conquer fear.

HOW TO WIN OVER PAIN
by *John Haggai*

With the same clear insight and powerful answers that made HOW TO WIN OVER WORRY a bestseller for more than 20 years, John Haggai addresses the problem of pain in our lives. Covering the gamut from physical suffering to the emotional anguish of rejection, loneliness, death, or separation, HOW TO WIN OVER PAIN asks the hard questions of life and presents God's strong and loving answers to our hurt and pain.

OVERCOMING HURTS AND ANGER
by *Dr. Dwight Carlson*

Dr. Carlson shows us how to confront our feelings and negative emotions in order to experience liberation and fulfillment. He presents seven practical steps to help us identify and cope with our feelings of hurt and anger.

PRIVATE PAIN
Healing for Hidden Hurts
by *Rich Wilkerson*

Rich Wilkerson, author of TEENAGERS: PARENTAL GUIDANCE SUGGESTED, tells us that "Few are exempt from some degree of private pain." Private pain may be emotional isolation, a sense of rejection, guilt, loneliness, depression, or other forms of inner anguish kept hidden from others. A book that offers help and understanding and shows how suffering and pain are the tools in the great Master Sculptor's plan for our lives.

THE PURPOSE OF SUFFERING
Knowing the God Who Comforts
by *Dr. H. Edwin Young*

A recent Gallup poll revealed that the most frequently asked question in America is, "Why do people suffer?" Dr. H. Edwin Young takes the reader through the book of Job for God's answer. He rejects the simplistic doctrines prevalent today that state, "You are suffering because of sin . . . God is punishing you!" and "As a child of God you can have complete health, wealth, and success just for the asking." Instead, he points the way to the sovereign God who alone can comfort us and show us THE PURPOSE OF SUFFERING.